Memoires of the Royal Navy 1690

Memoires
of the
Royal Navy
1690

SAMUEL PEPYS

NEW INTRODUCTION BY
J D DAVIES

Naval Institute Press
MARYLAND

Seaforth
PUBLISHING

Introduction copyright © J D Davies 2010

This edition first published in Great Britain in 2010 by
Seaforth Publishing,
Pen & Sword Books Ltd,
47 Church Street,
Barnsley S70 2AS

www.seaforthpublishing.com

And in the United States of America and Canada by
Naval Institute Press,
291 Wood Road, Annapolis,
Maryland 21402-5034

British Library Cataloguing in Publication Data
A catalogue record for this book is available from the British Library

Library of Congress Control No. 2009942411

ISBN 978 1 84832 065 9

The main text is a facsimile of the 1906 Clarendon Press edition,
which itself was typeset in the style of the original 1690 version.

Typeset by M.A.T.S., Southend-on-Sea, Essex

Printed and bound in Great Britain by Cromwell Press Group

NEW INTRODUCTION

THE *Memoires of the Royal Navy*, published in a single edition in about June 1690 and (apparently) chiefly circulated privately[1], was the only work written by Samuel Pepys to be published during his own lifetime. This was more by accident than by design; Pepys always intended to produce a detailed history of the Anglo-Dutch wars, a discrete work which eventually became subsumed into a project to write a much more ambitious naval history of England, but although he carried out much research for it, the great tome was never written[2]. Of course, the work for which he is best known, the diary that he kept between 1 January 1660 and 31 May 1669, was never intended for the sight of any other contemporary (especially his wife), let alone for wider dissemination in published form[3].

Despite the reflective nature of its title, the *Memoires* was not a ruminative work. It was conceived and executed very rapidly as a contribution to a partisan battle in which the author was deeply involved, and as such, it employed techniques of 'spin' that would have done credit to the politicians and administrators of any age. Its roots lay in the complex history of the Admiralty during the thirty years preceding its publication. From 1660 to 1673, the office of Lord High Admiral had been filled by King Charles II's brother and heir, James, Duke of York and Albany, with Pepys serving as Clerk of the Acts to the Navy Board, the body that undertook the day-to-day administration of the navy. James's conversion to Catholicism eventually forced his resignation in 1673; it also ensured that those who were closely associated with James, such as Pepys, were regarded with suspicion by those in Parliament and the country at large who opposed the perceived drift towards 'popery'. From 1673 to 1679 Charles II acted as his own Lord High Admiral, assisted by a commission which Pepys in theory served as Secretary, although in practice he acted more as the naval secretary to the king himself. This administrative structure then became a casualty of the 'Popish Plot' of 1678. In the following spring, Charles bowed to pressure from Parliament and installed an Admiralty commission of Parliamentarians, many of whom had built their reputations as opponents of naval spending. This body was soon given the full powers of a Lord High Admiral and embarked on a severe programme of naval retrenchment. In 1684, however, Charles was able to do away with a commission that he had always resented and reinstalled himself as Lord High Admiral *de jure*, with James acting *de facto*. Pepys became the first and (as it transpired) only holder of the exalted new office of Secretary for the Affairs of the Admiralty of England, essentially a naval minister modelled on the French pattern, and continued in the post when James succeeded to the throne on 6 February 1685. The overthrow of James in the 'Glorious Revolution' of 1689 also ended Pepys's tenure, and he left office in March 1689. Once again, the Admiralty passed to a board composed primarily of Parliamentarians and long-term opponents of the policies that James and Pepys had sought to implement[4].

Publication of the *Memoires* took place during the early stages of the 'Nine Years' War' against France. The new king,

William III, had seen the control of the fleet as one of his key objectives in invading England and ousting his father-in-law James, but the performance of that fleet during the first few months of the conflict was less than satisfactory. An engagement with the French in Bantry Bay on 1 May 1689 was at best a draw, although a government desperate to put the best possible gloss on the result immediately bestowed an earldom on the officer in command, Admiral Arthur Herbert, the new First Lord of the Admiralty and one of Pepys's bitterest opponents[5]. Charges of incompetent leadership and of providing inadequate equipment were bandied about, with Tories and crypto-Jacobites like Pepys damning the new regime and Whigs and others associated with the administration blaming the situation inherited from their predecessors. At the behest of his old friend John Evelyn, Pepys hastily dictated a defence of his time in office, and this eventually became the *Memoires.* Evelyn was fulsome in his praise of the author, and vitriolic on the subject of Pepys's enemies:

> With what indignation and folly, sorrow and contempt of their malice and ingratitude, do I look upon and despise them! On the other side, in what bonds and obligations of love, esteem and just admiration, ought we to regard him who dares expose himself to all this suffering with so intrepid a resolution...[6]

Others saw the *Memoires* rather differently. Its wealth of detail made it potentially valuable for opponents of the Williamite regime, and a copy was found among the papers of the Jacobite conspirator Viscount Preston as he attempted to flee the country on New Year's Day 1691[7]. The confidence of

Pepys and Evelyn that the little book would present an unanswerable case initially seemed misplaced, for Pepys's version of events was challenged by a lengthy parliamentary investigation carried out during 1691–2. The *Memoires* was cited as a source during that process; indeed, at least some of the enquiries undertaken by the MPs were couched as overt attempts to challenge some of the statements made in the *Memoires*, for instance by claiming that Pepys might have used 'means of terror' to obtain opinions that supported his case from the dockyard shipwrights[8]. Ultimately, though, the investigation concluded that Pepys's facts and figures were broadly correct, and these conclusions have been supported by more recent analysis[9]. However, it is also possible that Pepys had in mind something rather more immediate than simply defending his own reputation and damning his opponents' record. The early months of 1690 had witnessed something of a political sea-change, with Pepys's bitterest opponents, the Whigs, being displaced by a Tory regime headed by the Earl of Nottingham. The Admiralty had been remodelled in January: Pepys's greatest enemy on the commission, William Sacheverell[10], had been removed, and Torrington was replaced as First Lord by the much more amenable figure of Thomas Herbert, eighth Earl of Pembroke. A number of men who had been tainted with Jacobitism were returning to office, so it is not inconceivable that despite his refusal to take the oaths to the new regime, Pepys was dreaming of an unlikely comeback; and even if he proved to be beyond the pale as far as the Williamite regime was concerned, it might have seemed not impossible that a recapitulation of Pepys's achievements might lead to a recall for some of his clients and friends.

Supported by an impressive-looking array of lists, transcripts of official documents, and statistics, the *Memoires* presents Pepys's argument that he left the navy in good order at his first departure from the Admiralty in 1679, that his incompetent successors then allowed it to go to wrack and ruin between 1679 and 1684, and that the far-sightedness of Pepys and King James II, particularly in the appointment of a special commission for naval reconstruction from 1686 to 1688, restored the navy to an excellent condition prior to his second departure from office in 1689. The bulk of the evidence in the *Memoires* was drawn from the report that Pepys had presented to King Charles II on 31 December 1684, barely five weeks before that monarch's death, and which Pepys read to the new King James on 10 February 1685, just four days after his accession; a new report was formally presented to James in January 1686 and became the catalyst for the creation of the 'special commission'[11].

Perhaps the most eye-catching evidence produced by Pepys concerns the size of the active fleet at each of the three key dates, 1679, 1684 and 1688. According to the *Memoires*, in the spring of 1679, seventy-six ships were at sea, carrying a total of some 12,040 men. When Pepys returned to the Admiralty in May 1684, however, he found only twenty-four ships carrying 3,070 men. This calamitous situation was rectified by the Special Commission, so that when this body was wound up in October 1688 sixty-seven ships were at sea, carrying 12,303 men. In fact, Pepys's deployment of these statistics displays a breathtakingly audacious disregard for the context. The large fleet at sea in 1679 was a legacy of the previous year's mobilisation for a war against France that ultimately never broke out; the ships were still in service only because the Admiralty that Pepys served lacked the funds to pay them off. The ships in service in 1684 represented a normal peacetime summer guard, and in fact thirty-nine ships were in service, not twenty-four; the much-derided commission of 1679–84 sent out about forty ships every summer, rather more on average than Pepys managed during both his stints at the Admiralty. The increased numbers in service in October 1688 were not a consequence of enlightened naval reconstruction *per se*; they represented the mobilisation against William of Orange's invasion and the defeat of all that Pepys stood for, rather than his triumph[12].

A similarly ingenious distortion of the record can be traced throughout the *Memoires*. Pepys claimed that at the time of the Duke of Monmouth's rebellion in 1685, only one Fourth Rate frigate could be mobilised to defend the coast; but his own letterbooks, which he had taken with him on leaving office, prove conclusively that he was involved in mobilising a far larger force that included three Third Rates, and that the only thing that prevented their deployment was the rapid defeat of the rebellion at the Battle of Sedgemoor[13]. Pepys devoted much attention to the royal order of 1686 that prohibited the practice of transporting bullion in warships, with a commission of one per cent going to the captain; Pepys had come to believe that this facility was deeply injurious to good discipline in the navy because it tempted captains to abandon their duties in order to seek lucrative plate cargoes, especially at Cadiz. Pepys's commendation of his own and King James's far-sightedness in ending this abuse and creating a new system of expenses that virtually doubled captains' pay overlooked the fact that the new allowances were never paid, and that plate carriage would survive in the Royal Navy until

1914[14]. Pepys had to employ particularly pronounced brass neck in justifying the composition of the Special Commission of 1686–8. His statement that King James had made his choice 'after a most solicitous enquiry made, and collection had of as many persons (and all, God knows, but few) as the navy of England could furnish him with...was pleas'd to fix his choice upon Sir Anthony Deane, Sir John Berry, Mr Hewer, [and] Mr St Michel' is actually a disingenuous defence of a singular piece of nepotism. Hewer had been Pepys's clerk and servant, eventually becoming one of his closest friends and, at the last, his executor, following Pepys's death in Hewer's house. The master shipwright Anthony Deane had been Pepys's friend since the 1660s; he had taught him many of the mysteries of shipbuilding and served with him as MP for Harwich. Berry had become friendly with Pepys during the expedition of Lord Dartmouth's fleet to Tangier in 1683–4, when Pepys had served as Dartmouth's secretary. Meanwhile Balthasar St Michel had served with varying degrees of competence in a series of lowly or middling naval posts during the preceding twenty years; there was nothing to qualify him for membership of such a small and important group, other than the fact that his late sister had been married to Samuel Pepys[15].

The centrepiece of the *Memoires* is the charge that the Admiralty Commission of 1679–84 had been responsible for a marked deterioration in the physical condition of the 'thirty new ships'. These vessels[16] had been built from 1677 onwards as a response to concerns over the rapid expansion of the French navy; Pepys had been largely responsible for persuading a suspicious House of Commons of the necessity to vote funds for their construction. However, the condition of the ships soon became a serious cause for concern. By 1681, neutral sources were commenting on their decay; by 1684 there was extensive evidence of rot. Pepys describes this in the most vivid terms: 'I have seen toad-stools growing in them as big as my fists; some never once heeled or breamed since their building but exposed in hot weather to the sun, broiling in their buttocks and elsewhere for want of liquoring and cooling them with water' (a description that apparently amused generations of officer cadets at Dartmouth[17], to whom it was being held up as an example of government neglect of the navy; *plus ça change*). Both at the time and in the *Memoires*, Pepys blamed the Admiralty for failing to undertake proper maintenance. In turn, the Admiralty's supporters lambasted Pepys and his regime for purchasing inferior Baltic timber instead of honest English oak, while also attacking the master shipwrights for building the ships too hastily[18]. The *Memoires* reports the outcome of a consultation with the shipwrights in 1686 at which they concurred with Pepys's line, and the most detailed recent study of the issue concludes that their assessment of the situation was largely correct: the chief cause of the deterioration was the inadequate maintenance provided by dockyard officers, particularly at Chatham[19]. For example, the sides and upper works of ships laid up 'in ordinary' were meant to be watered every morning and evening from May to August, but this was not done on a number of the thirty ships, notably the Second Rates *Vanguard* and *Ossory*, laid up at Portsmouth[20]. However, Pepys's attempt to throw all the blame for this onto his rivals in the Admiralty commission of 1679–84 (and, by extension, that of 1689 onwards) deliberately ignored undoubtedly the most important cause for the lack of proper maintenance. Between 1679 and 1684 the Admiralty was very much a subordinate body. It was the largest spending department of the state at a time when severe retrenchment of public expenditure was taking place, primarily because Charles II wished to ensure that he did not have to depend for finance on a Parliament that was determined to vote for the exclusion of his brother from the succession. Therefore the Treasury was given virtually unprecedented control over expenditure, and it sought to rein in the Admiralty above all.

Limited to just £300,000 a year and saddled with debts that it had inherited from the previous (Pepysian) regime, the Admiralty of 1679–84 had no alternative but to implement a series of cutbacks and economies. There is ample evidence that it warned the Treasury many times of the deteriorating condition of the thirty ships and of the disastrous consequences of allowing the pay of the ships and dockyards to slip ever further into arrears, but these appeals fell largely on deaf ears. However, Pepys chose to ignore this context when he came to write the *Memoires*. It hardly fitted with his own political agenda: identifying the Treasury as the true cause of naval decay would have weakened his case against the Admiralty itself, while he could hardly criticise the Treasury without implicitly or explicitly criticising the men who had dictated its course of action, namely King Charles II and (later) his brother James, both of whom were above criticism in Pepys's eyes (or at least, above criticism in documents for public consumption; Pepys's private notes made much of the Stuart brothers' erratic policies and inconsistent stance on discipline). In fact, it was not until eighteen months after he became Secretary for the Affairs of the Admiralty of England that Pepys was able to launch his 'special commission' and the programme for naval reconstruction; not because of the death of Charles II, as he claimed, but because it took that long for funds to come through from the enthusiastically royalist Parliament elected after the accession of James II[21].

The *Memoires* is not great literature: unwieldy language, the bane of many of Pepys's official letters (yet generally absent from his lively diary), was exacerbated in this case by the fact that the work was dictated[22]. It is also not great history, at least not by modern standards. But then, Pepys's attitude to writing 'history' was unequivocal and entirely typical of his times. Those attributes praised by modern historians, notably neutrality and objectivity, were noticeable only by their absence; instead, Pepys saw the writing of history un-ashamedly as a weapon in a polemical battleground. His thoughts on his proposed history of the Anglo-Dutch wars reveal this clearly. After explaining how he would carry out commendably extensive research (examining both private and public state correspondence, studying captains' journals, interviewing both English and Dutch ministers, and so on) Pepys entirely prejudged the conclusions to be drawn from such research by stating that all 'which particulars put together in this or some such order will undoubtedly vindicate the right of His Majesty's arms, and throw all the scandal of our differences on the artifice or treachery of [Dutch Grand Pensionary Johan] De Witt'[23].

Pepys's manipulation of the record in the *Memoires* was similarly deliberate, and carried out for overtly political ends. Therefore the many historians who have treated *Pepys's Memoires* as a judicious and ultimately correct assessment of naval affairs between about 1673 and 1690 have fallen into the trap carefully laid for them by the ingenious Mr Pepys[24]. One of those who did so was Joseph Robson Tanner (1860–1931), who was responsible for the most recent edition of the *Memoires* (published by Clarendon Press in 1906). A fellow and tutor at St John's College, Cambridge, Tanner was an unashamed enthusiast for Pepys and all his works[25]. He even believed that it was possible to write the history of the Restoration navy entirely from Pepys's papers at Magdalene College, Cambridge, a mentality shaped as much by the then (and, to some extent, still) chaotic nature of the naval sources at other repositories as by geographical inertia[26]. Tanner's introduction to the 1906 edition provides an excellent example of how successfully Pepys gulled not only his contemporaries, but also many succeeding generations.

The *Memoires of the Royal Navy* thus constitutes a fascinating object lesson in the manipulation of statistics and the historical record for political ends. Pepys unashamedly distorted the record to exaggerate his own reputation and to damn the reputations of his opponents; he certainly would not be the last senior civil servant or government minister to do so. It is therefore possible to trace a clear thread of continuity from the Pepys of the 'diary period', who always produced a barrage of evidence and statistics to batter his opponents into submission (for instance, in his famous defence of the Navy Board before the House of Commons on 5 March 1668). At the last, the *Memoires of the Royal Navy* certainly provides a vivid insight into the state of the navy in the 1680s, but more importantly, it stands as one of the best memorials to the ingenuity and sheer political cunning of Samuel Pepys.

J D Davies, 2010

NOTES

1. The 'public' version of the work was printed for Benjamin Griffin and sold by Samuel Keble; a variant imprint gave no information other than the year of printing (cf C S Knighton, *Pepys and the Navy* (Stroud, 2003), 194, n 3). A facsimile edition of the *Memoires*, edited by J R Tanner, was published by Oxford University Press in 1906. However, the work was clearly not circulated to friends alone; in 2009 a bookseller was advertising the copy acquired on 20 May 1691 by the Whig politician William Sacheverell, a prominent opponent of Pepys (www.abebooks.co.uk, accessed 3 September 2009, offered for sale by Christopher Edwards of Wallingford, Oxfordshire).
2. See Pepys's allusion in the conclusion of the *Memoires* to a *'Navalia'* or general naval history. Many of his research notes and memoranda were subsequently published as *Samuel Pepys's Naval Minutes*, ed. E Chappell (Navy Records Society, 1925). Cf Knighton, *Pepys and the Navy*, 163–4.
3. Thus the many 'bloggers' who claim Pepys as one of their own miss the point entirely; publishing his innermost thoughts and deeds to the world in his own lifetime would have been utter anathema to him.
4. J D Davies, *Pepys's Navy: Ships, Men and Warfare 1649–89* (Barnsley, 2008), 25–8.
5. The antipathy was reciprocated; Pepys's vitriolic notes on Herbert's command of the Mediterranean fleet from 1679 to 1683 eventually found their way into print as *The Tangier Papers of Samuel Pepys*, ed J R Tanner (Navy Records Society, 1935).
6. Evelyn to Pepys, 11 June 1690, quoted by C Tomalin, *Samuel Pepys: The Unequalled Self* (2002), 358.
7. Preston's copy is now at the Folger Shakespeare Library, call number P1450; I am grateful to Peter Le Fevre for this reference.
8. Historical Manuscripts Commission, *Report on the Manuscripts of the Duke of Portland, Preserved at Welbeck Abbey*, X (1931), 7. Cf British Library, Additional MS 70,035, fo. 113, Hewer to Commissioners of Public Accounts, 12 Aug. 1691 (I am grateful to Frank Fox for drawing my attention to these references).
9. Knighton, *Pepys and the Navy*, 153–4.
10. S Handley, 'Sacheverell, William (1637/8–1691), politician', *Oxford Dictionary of National Biography* (2004).

11. Magdalene College, Cambridge, Pepys MS 1534, p. 51 and passim; Pepys MS 1490, pp. 81–121. In turn, the reports were based on the notes in such sources as Bodleian Library, Oxford, Rawlinson MS A464.

12. See my 'Pepys and the Admiralty Commission of 1679–84', *Historical Research* 62 (1989), 43-4.

13. Magdalene College, Cambridge, Pepys MS 2858, pp. 24–198.

14. *Pepys's Navy*, 105.

15. For Berry, Deane and Hewer, see the entries in *ODNB*; for St Michel, see Tomalin, *Samuel Pepys*, 56–7, 98, 109, 113, 183, 250, 295, 296, 319, 321, 322, 328, 334, 344, 355, 359. The circumstances surrounding the creation and composition of the commission are well covered by Knighton, *Pepys and the Navy*, 148–50. The positive side of such an obviously nepotistic set of appointments is that the men concerned were personally loyal to Pepys, and could be guaranteed to work together to implement his agenda.

16. One First Rate, the *Britannia*; nine Seconds; and twenty Thirds. The last ship in the programme was not actually launched until 1685.

17. Knighton, *Pepys and the Navy*, 148.

18. Davies, 'Pepys and the Admiralty Commission', 44.

19. R Endsor, *The Restoration Warship: The Design, Construction and Career of a Third Rate of Charles II's Navy* (2009), 128–46, 242–4. I am grateful to Richard Endsor for many discussions on this subject.

20. *Pepys's Navy*, 72.

21. The question of the relative roles of the Treasury and Admiralty, and of Pepys's interpretation of both, is examined in greater detail in my 'Pepys and the Admiralty Commission', 44–52.

22. Tomalin, *Samuel Pepys*, 358.

23. Bodleian Library, Oxford, Rawlinson MS A185, fo. 222. For other examples of Pepys setting out to use history to 'prove' a predetermined conclusion, see C S Knighton, 'Pepys and the Elizabethan Navy', *TRHS*, 14 (2004), 149–50.

24. Most notably Sir Arthur Bryant and Richard Ollard. Cf the former's *Samuel Pepys: The Saviour of the Navy* (1938) and the latter's *Pepys: A Biography* (1974),

25. A good biographical article on him, by E A Benians and revised by K D Reynolds, appears in the *Oxford Dictionary of National Biography*.

26. Tanner (ed.), *A Descriptive Catalogue of the Naval Manuscripts in the Pepysian Library at Magdalene College, Cambridge*, i (Navy Records Society, 1903), 3. An excellent account of the infuriatingly irrational 'organisation' of other naval archives, in marked contrast to the highly logical system developed by Pepys for his library at Magdalene, is provided by N A M Rodger, 'Drowning in a Sea of Paper: British Archives of Naval Warfare', *Archives*, 32 (2007), 104–11.

𝕸𝖊𝖒𝖔𝖎𝖗𝖊𝖘

Relating to the

S T A T E

OF THE

ROYAL NAVY

O F

E N G L A N D,

For Ten Years, Determin'd
December 1688.

---

*Quantis molestiis vacant, qui nihil omninò
cum Populo contrahunt ? Quid Dulcius
Otio Litterato ?* Cic. Tusc. Disp.

L O N D O N:

Printed for *Ben. Griffin,* and are to be sold
by *Sam. Keble* at the Great *Turks-Head* in
Fleet-street over against *Fetter-Lane,* 1690.

𝔐𝔢𝔪𝔬𝔦𝔯𝔢𝔰

Relating to the

STATE

OF THE

ROYAL NAVY

OF

ENGLAND.

'TWas in *April* 1679, when (my April
unhappy *Master,* his then *Royal* 1679
Highness, having but newly been
commanded abroad, and my self now
shut up in the *Tower*) *His Majesty* K. *Admi-*
Charles the Second was led to the ex- *ralty-*
changing the *Method,* wherein the *Manage-*
Affairs of his *Admiralty* had for some *ment*
years before been manag'd under his *altered.*
own Inspection, for that of a *Com-*
mission, charg'd with the *Execution* of
the whole *Office* of his *High Admiral.*

An *Occurrence* carrying this in it of peculiar; That no one *Article* of *Time* appears within the whole *History* of our *Navy*, wherein this could have fallen out more equally towards the *Persons* immediately interested in the *Alteration*. Forasmuch as (by occasion of a *War* then newly in agitation with *France*) the *State* of the *Navy* had past an *Inquisition* so publick and solemn (extant at this day in the *Registers* both of *Parliament* and its own) as no time can shew to have at once been ever before taken; leaving no room for Controversie (under any future *Events*) touching the condition wherein the *Navy* was at that time, either deliver'd over by the *one*, or taken in charge by the *other*.

Which Condition *was shortly this,* viz.

I. The *Gross* of the *Fleet* of *England* was in that state of *Repair*, as (in prospect of the foremention'd *War*) to have had but few Months before, and upon less than four Months warning,

ing, actually in *Sea-service* and *Pay*,
compleatly furnished with six Months
Sea-stores, Eighty three of His *Majesties*
own *Ships* of *War* and *Fire-Ships* (over
and above Merchant-men, and the
numerous Train of *Ketches, Smacks,
Yachts,* and other small Craft, attending the same) and these of the highest,
as well as other Rates, employing in
the whole above 18000 Men, as follows.

𝕬𝖇𝖘𝖙𝖗𝖆𝖈𝖙 *of the* 𝕱𝖑𝖊𝖊𝖙 *in* August, 1678.

		Nº	Men.
	1	5	3135
	2	4	1555
Rates	3	16	5010
	4	33	6460
	5	12	1400
	6	7	423
Fire-Ships		6	340
	Total	83	18323

Of which were left in like *Sea-Pay*
at the time of my *Confinement,* Threescore

ſcore and Sixteen of the following
Rates, bearing 12000 Men.

𝕬𝖇𝖘𝖙𝖗𝖆𝖈𝖙 *of the* 𝕱𝖑𝖊𝖊𝖙, *left by Mr.*
Pepys *in* Sea-pay, April 1679.

Nº

$$
\text{Rates} \left\{
\begin{array}{ll}
1 & ---\ 1 \\
2 & ---\ 3 \\
3 & ---15 \\
4 & ---30 \\
5 & ---12 \\
6 & ---\ 7
\end{array}
\right\}
\begin{array}{l}
\textit{Men.} \\
---12040
\end{array}
$$

Fire-Ships ——— 8

Total 76

Condition
of thoſe
in Har-
bour.
II. The whole *Reſidue* of the *King's*
Repairable *Ships* were (upon no leſs
ſolemn an *Enquiry*) reported within
the ſame time, by the *Surveyor* of his
Navy, and *Body* of the *Navy-Board,*
in a condition of being throughly
fitted for the *Sea* and furniſh'd with
Sea-ſtores for 50000 *l.*

Stores in
Maga-
zine.
III. And towards this, and the
anſwering what extraordinary *Supplies*
this

this *Fleet* (had not the War prov'd abortive, and the *Ships* with their *Stores* been thereby in the main foon brought in and laid up) might have had occafion for, beyond its fore-mention'd fix Months; a further *Re-ferve* remain'd untoucht in *Magazine*, to the value of *Threefcore thoufand pounds*.

IV. Laftly, A *Force* additional to all this of Thirty *Capital Ships* was then actually in *Building*; Whereof Eleven newly *Launch'd*, and the Re-mainder (all of them) under an affidu-ous profecution upon the *Stocks*. An Addition, rendering the *Whole* a Se-curity not unequal (ordinary *Providence* concurring) to the publick *Ends* of it, in the maintenance of the *Peace* and *Honour* of the *Government* on *Shore*, and fupport of its ancient, rightful, and envy'd *Title* to *Dominion* at *Sea*.

Thirty Capital Ships in Building.

This was the *Pofture* of the *Royal Navy* at the time of my *Removal* from it. Concerning which I fhall take

the

the liberty only to fay, That though I am one, who could never think any room left for a *Subject's* Supererogating in the honeft *Service* of his *Prince*; yet cannot I but own fo much content in the contemplation of that little *Part* I had born in the rendring it

State of the Navy of Eng- land in no time better.

fuch, as may reafonably arife from the not being confcious of any one *Inftance* to be fhewn me through the whole *Marine Hiftory* of *England*, of a time wherein its *Navy* had been ever before recorded in a better.

May 1679, Commif- fion of the Ad- miralty, its Date and Dur- ation.

And fo fets out this *Commiffion* in *May* 1679, continuing in its Execution five years.

During which, being my felf wholly fequeftred from that and all other *Publick Affairs*, Thofe of the *Navy* became foreign to me; as having no other Notices concerning them, than what too often occurr'd in common converfation, touching the *effects* of

Conduct thereof obferved.

Inexperience daily difcovering them- felves in their *Conduct*; and (what was no mean *Addition* to it) the unconcern-
ment

ment wherewith his then *Majesty* was said to suffer his being familiarly entertain'd on that Subject; while at the same time his transcendent *Mastery* in all *Maritime* [1] *Knowledge*, could not (upon the least *Reflection*) but bring into his view, the serious *Reckoning* the same must soon or late end in, to his *Purse* and *Government*. As at the five *years* end it prov'd to do.

When (in *May* 1684.) being self-convinc'd of the inexpediency of his longer continuing the *Navy* under that *Management*, He was pleas'd to come to a sudden determination, of resuming the Business of it into his own *Hands*, assisted by his *Royal Brother* then come back, and by his Commands, (neither sought-for, nor foreseen, but brought me expresly from *Windsor* by the Lord *Dartmouth*) to require my immediate Return to the *Post* I had formerly had the *Honour* of serving him at, therein.

Pursuant hereto, the late *Commission* being

May 1684.

Navy resumed into the Kings own hands, assisted by his R.H.

Mr. Pepys recalled.

Admi-raltyCom-mission dissolved.

[1] *Maritime corr.* S. P.

A Review of the Navy as returned to the King, here stated.

Ships at Sea.

being diſſolv'd, and His *Majeſty* taking to himſelf the Perſonal *Direction* of its *Work*; He judg'd it for his *Service* to begin with a freſh *Enquiry* into the *Condition* wherein his *Navy* was now return'd him, and found the *Reſult* of it this.

I. *Four and Twenty* of his *Ships* (and no more) were then at *Sea*, and thoſe of the following *Rates* (not one above a fourth) employing but 3070 *Men*.

Abſtract *of the* **Fleet** *at* Sea *at the* Cloſe *of the* Commiſſion *of the* Admiralty, May 1684.

		Nº.	Men.
Rates—	4ᵗʰ.	12	2120
	5	5	560
	6	5	325
Fire Ships		2	65
	Total	24	3070

Condition of thoſe in Harbour.

II. The *Remainder* of the *Navy* in *Harbour* ſo far out of *Repair*, as to have had the *Charge* of that alone (without *Sea-Stores*) eſtimated juſt before

fore by the fame *Surveyor* and *Board*, at no lefs than *One hundred and twenty thoufand Pounds.*

III. And towards this, a *Magazine* of *Stores*, as lately reported from the fame *Hands*, not to amount to *Five thoufand Pounds.*

A *Magazine*, fo unequal to the Oc-cafions of fuch a *Navy*; that whereas *Peace* us'd evermore to be improv'd to the making up the *wafteful effects* of *War*. This appears (after the longeft *Vacation* of a *Home-marine Peace*, from the *Reftauration* of the *King* to this *Day*) to have brought the *Navy* into a *ftate*, more deplorable in its *Ships*, and lefs relievable from its *Stores*, than can be fhewn to have happen'd (either in the *One*, or the *Other*) at the *Clofe* of the moft expenceful *War*, within all that time, or in *forty years* before.

IV. *Efpecially*, when in this its *General* ill plight, confideration fhall be had of that *Particular* therein, which relates to the *Thirty New Ships*. Not

more

Maga-zine.

That Maga-zine con-fidered.

Ill State of the 30 *New Ships.*

more furprizing for the *Fact*, (after the folemnity and ampleneſs of the *Proviſion* made for them by *Parliament*) than important for its *Conſequences.*

Import of thoſe Ships. Foraſmuch as in theſe Ships refted not only that, by which the preſent *Sea-ſtrength* of *England* furmounted all it had ever before had to pretend to, and the utmoft that its preſent *Woods* (at leaſt within any reaſonable *Reach* of its *Arſenals*) feem now able to fup-port with *Materials*, or its *Navigation* with *Men*; but that *Portion* alſo of the fame, upon which alone may at this day be rightfully faid to reft, the *virtue* of the *whole*, oppos'd to the no leſs confiderable *Growths* in the *Naval ſtrengths* of *France* and *Holland.*

The ill-neſs of their State par-ticular-ized. The greateſt part neverthelefs of theſe *Thirty Ships* (without having ever yet lookt out of *Harbour*) were let to fink into fuch Diftrefs, through *Decays* contracted in their *Buttocks, Quarters, Bows, Thick-ſtuff* without *Board*, and *Spir-kettings* upon their *Gun-decks* with-in; their *Buttock-Planks* fome of them
ſtarted

started from their *Transums*, *Tree-nails*
burnt and rotted, and *Planks* thereby
become ready to drop into the *Water*,
as being (with their Neighbouring
Timbers) in many places perish'd to
powder, to the rendring them unable
with safety to admit of being *breem'd*,
for fear of taking *Fire*; and their
whole *sides* more disguis'd by *Shot-
boards* nail'd, and *Plaisters* of *Canvas*
pitch'd thereon (for hiding their *Defects*, and keeping them above *Water*)
than has been usually seen upon the
coming in of a *Fleet* after a *Battle*;
that several of them had been newly
reported by the *Navy-Board* it self, to
lye in danger of *sinking* at their very
Moorings.

And *this*, notwithstanding above
Six hundred thousand pounds (not yet
accounted for by the *Navy-Board*)
spent in their *Building* and *Furniture*,
with above *Threescore and ten thousand
pounds* more demanded for compleating them, amounting together to
670000 *l.*; and therein *exceeding*, not
only

Excessive Charge of these Ships, un-accounted for.

only the *Navy Officers* own *Estimates*, and their *Master-Ship-wrights Demands*, but even the *Charge* which some of them appear'd to have been actually *built for*, by above *One hundred* and *seventy thousand pounds.*

The Fond for them well answered.
And notwithstanding too, the flowing in of the *Monies* provided for them by *Parliament*, faster (for the most part) than their *Occasions* of employing it.

Provisions for securing an Account of these Ships, yet ineffectual.
In a word ; notwithstanding the *strict Provision* made by *Parliament*, the repeated *Injunctions* of His *Majesty*, the *Orders* of the then *Lord Treasurer*, and ampleness of the *Helps* purposely allow'd (to the full of their own *Demands and Undertakings*) for securing a satisfactory *Account* of the *Charge* and *Built* of the said *Ships.*

400000l. per Annum paid the Navy all this while.
V. *Lastly*, While the *Navy* (under this five *years* uninterrupted *Peace*) was suffer'd to sink into this calamitous estate, even to the rendring some of its *Number* wholly *irrepairable*, and reducing others (the most considerable
in

in *Quality*) to a *Condition* of being with difficulty kept above *Water*; the *Navy* (as His *Majesty* was then affur'd by the *Lord Treasurer*) had been all that while fupply'd, (one year with another) with *Four hundred thousand Pounds* per Ann.

Which being then the *Condition* of the *Navy*, and (as fuch) not receptive of any fenfible *Amendment* within the fhort remainder of the *Life* of *King Charles*; his *Royal Brother* King *James* (upon his coming to the *Throne* in *February* following) was pleas'd to take among the firft of his *Cares* this of the *Navy*, by an immediate appli-cation to the animating and enabling its *Officers* (with fuitable Supplies of *Money*) to an induftrious and effectual *beftirring* themfelves towards the *re-dreffing* it. *Death of K. Charles, Febr. 1684. K. James falls im-mediately upon the redrefs of the Navy, by the Officers thereof.*

But with fuch unfuccefsfulnefs (after a whole *year's* Proof of their *Perform-ances*) as upon a frefh *View* of its *State*, taken in *January* 168⅚, to difcover it felf ftill declin'd to a yet more *But after a years proof wholly unfuccefs-ful.*

deplor-

State of the Na-vy, Janu-ary, 1685.

deplorable degree of *Calamity* ; as follows,

I. After the *Expence* in *Workmanſhip* and *Materials* of above *Ninety thouſand Pounds,* the *Navy-Officers* ſtill demand for the *Repairs* of the *Fleet* the very ſame *Sum* the *Works* had by themſelves been valu'd at, before a *Penny* of that *Ninety thouſand pounds* had been laid out.

90000 *l.* ſpent fruitleſly.

Ships not Graved.

II. Not a *Quarter* of the *Ships* grav'd, which *themſelves* had propos'd the having done within that time, and been expreſly ſupply'd with the *Monies* demanded for it.

No Ships in preſent readineſs for Ser-vice upon an Exi-gence.

III. But one fourth *Rate,* and not ſo much as one *Fifth,* found (in the *Exigence* of the *Duke* of *Monmouth*'s *Invaſion*) in a condition of being got to *Sea,* in leſs than two *Months,* but by robbing of the very *Harbour-Guard.*

The 30 *New Ships not yet gone in hand with,*

IV. Several of the 30 *Ships* (re-ported near two years ſince in a condition of *ſinking*) not yet ſo much as gone in hand with, though *Money* ex-

exprefly fupply'd for that ufe too, by *Though* the Lord Treafurer. *Money*

V. Their *Stores* alfo of greateft *value*, and calling for moft time to provide (fuch as *Cables, Sails,* &c.) fo much wanting, either through *Decay,* or being (in neglect of the *Statute*) diverted to *other ufes,* as not to have any one of them furnifh'd for the *Sea,* had they been otherwife in *Condition* for it.

fupply'd.

Their Stores alfo wanting.

VI. *Twice* as much time now demanded for fitting out *forty two* Ships, as had a year and half fince been ask'd for *fifty five.*

The Time asked for fitting out Ships, more than doubled.

VII. Not the leaft *Provifion* made of *Long Timber* or *Plank,* for anfwering the moft preffing and weighty works of the *Growing year;* though the greateft Part of the *Money* demanded for that ufe alfo, had been actually *advanc'd,* and the *Refidue* lay in a known readinefs to be fo, as faft as call'd for.

No Provifion made of the moft neceffary Materials, though Money fupply'd for that alfo.

VIII. *Three Years* ftill infifted on for the *Repair* of the *Fleet,* while *five* Months

Time length-

ened be-
yond
measure
for repair
of the
Fleet.

Months only rested unexpir'd of the time, within which (by former *Calculations* of their own) the *whole* was to have been *finish'd.*

Notwith-
standing
all Helps,
the Fleets
decays
outgrow
their
Cure.

IX. *Lastly*, After the utmost *proofs* of the *Procedures* of this *Board*, assisted by *Money* to the height of their *Demands*, it seem'd manifest to *His Majesty*, that the *Fleet's Decays* outgrew their *Cure*; and that should no other *course* be found for the remedying it, than what was now *stirring* among the

Navy
Officers
Estimates
of Repairs
incon-
sistent.

Navy Officers (whose *Estimates* of the very same *date* were found sometimes to differ not less than *double*, nay even *treble*, in the *Charge* of the *Repairs* of the very same *Ship*) no time could be

Nor any
time to be
depended
on for the
dispatch
thereof.

assign'd, within which (if ever) their *Decays* (even as they then stood, without ought allow'd for their greatnings by *Delay*) could have their *Repairs* depended on.

Causes of
these
Evils
what,
and what
not.

From whence, and from the *King's* being in an especial manner convinc'd, that no part of these *Evils* sprang from the want of *Money*, *Hands*, *Materials*

or

or *Time*, but from other *Imperfections*, obvious enough, but uneafie to be now rectify'd in the *Perfons* principally accountable for them ; and confidering likewife the neceffity of having fome inftant and effectual *Some in-* *Remedy* provided, e're the *mifchiefs* *ftant* *Remedy* attending this *Management* became *neceffary.* (what *one years* delay more muft, at leaft as to the New Ships, have render'd them) infuperable : He was pleas'd (in fubferviency to his own) to require my *Thoughts* touching the *Methods* moft likely to compafs his *Royal Aim* herein, and how far that (with the other ftanding and indif- penfable *Charges* of his *Navy* at *Sea* *To be* and in *Harbour*) might be together *(with the* *other* anfwer'd with 400000 *l. per Annum* ; *neceffary* the Sum the then *Lord Treafurer* firft *charges of* propofed the way of providing, and *the Na-* the *King* his Readinefs to have fet *vy) de-* entirely apart for it. *frayed* *with*

Which accordingly I foon after 400000l. prefented him with, in the *Terms* per Ann. following.

To the *KING*.

Sir,

THough the general and habitual supineſs, waſtefulneſs *and* neglect *of* Order *univerſally ſpread through your whole* Navy, with the No-proviſion *yet made of Materials the moſt neceſſary and difficult to be found for this ſo great* Work; *adding thereto the impoſſibility of arriving at any perfect knowledge of the* weight *of that* work, *from the diſagreements daily diſcovered between the* Eſtimates *and real* Charge *of* Works *when perform'd*; *and laſtly, the heavy conſequences of any* Failure *that may happen in its Execution, ſeem to render any peremptory* undertaking herein (*from* me *at leaſt*) *very unſafe, if at all juſtifiable.* Yet *ſo much am I acquainted with the Power of* Induſtry *and* Good Husbandry, *joyn'd with* Knowledg *and* Methodical Application (*no two of which ſeem at this day ſtirring together in any Part of your* Naval Service) *that after weighing every Article of what I am by your* Majeſty's

Tender of undertaking ought.

Com-

*Command now going to offer you, I am
satisfy'd that your* Majesty *may reasonably
expect the services mention'd in the following* Proposition, *Viz.*

Proposition.

That *with* 400000 l. per Annum, *supply'd by* 100000 *l. within each* Quarter,
and in a known and effectual Order *of*
Payments, *to be pre-adjusted with the*
Persons, *who (being rightly* [1] *qualify'd
for it) shall be intrusted by your* Majesty,
with the Management *thereof, and assisted
with your* Authority *in all matters conducing to the* Recovery *of the lost*
Discipline *and* Industry *of your* Navy;
the Retrenchment *of all unnecessary*
Charges *and* Wastes; *the encouraging
and improving all means of* Good Husbandry *and reasonable* savings; *and
the due* Correction *of all* misdoers *in
any of the* Premisses; *your* Majesty *may
expect the* Effects *following, Viz.*

I. The whole ordinary charge *of*
your Navy *on* Shore *and in* Harbour
to be fully defray'd, and therein the
Hulls

*Mr.
Pepys's
Proposition.*

400000*l.
the Fund
assign'd
for it,
with the
conditions
of the
Proposition.*

*Ordinary
charge
and
works*

[1] *rightfully corr.* S. P.

Hulls *of your* Ships *duly kept in their*
ordinary Repair, *grav'd (as by the*
Rules *of the* Navy *they ought always
to have been) by one* Third *every* year,
and supply'd with Ground Tackle *fuf-
ficient for their safe* mooring; *and your*
Offices *alfo and* dwelling Houfes, Store-
Houfes, Wharfes, Cranes, *and* Keys *to
be throughout put into, and kept in their*
Ordinary repair.

II. The extraordinary Decays *under
which the* Body *of your whole* Fleet in
Harbour *now lies, to receive the full of
their* Repair *alfo, to the utmoft of what
has been yet difcover'd and defcribed in
the laft and higheft* Surveys *and* Eftimates
prefented of them to your Majefty *by your*
Navy Officers, *amounting
(with their* Stores) *to* 220000*l.;
and this (with the finifhing
the* Three New 4*th.* Rates)
to be compleated *within the* year

l.
Repaires — 132000
Sea-Stores- 88000
Tot — 220000

*Within
what
time, and
how to
be per-
formed.*

1688.; *and fo done, that your* Majefty
and your Lord Treafurer *may (according
to the ancient and rightful* Methods *of
the* Navy) *be fatisfy'd at the end of each*
fer-

ſervice, *how the* Charge *thereof has concurr'd with, exceeded, or fallen ſhort of their* Eſtimates, *and the* Monies *ſav'd there-from be made good to your* Majeſty, *where too much ; or the* ſervice *further provided for by* ſupplimental Eſtimates, *where the firſt has fail'd of anſwering the* real Charge.

III. *Theſe* Ships (*as faſt as repair'd and fitted in their* Hulls) *to be in like manner compleatly ſupply'd with ſix* Months Sea-Stores, *and thoſe ſeparately laid up and preſerv'd for uſe, whenever the* Service *of their reſpective* Ships *ſhall* call *for them.* *To be furniſhed with Sea-Stores.*

IV. '*The ſame Number of* Ships, *and of equal* Rates *with those deſign'd by your* Majeſty *in your late* Declaration *for* 3000 *Men for the preſent* year, *to be maintain'd at* Sea *in their full* Wages, Victuals, Wear *and* Tear, *for anſwering all your* Foreign Occaſions ; *With this* Addition, *that for the advancing*[1] *the* Honour *of your* Majeſty *and your* Government, *and the* maintenance *of your* Right *of* Sovereignty *in theſe* Seas,

[1] *advaning corr.* S. P.

Seas, *beyond what appears to have been ever yet provided for it in time of* Peace; *your* Majesty *may* (*instead of the three* small Ships *design'd by that* Declaration *for your whole* Channel-Guard, *mann'd but with* 275 Men) *have a Squadron of ten* Ships, *consisting of one* 3d. *four* 4th. *three* 5th. *and two* 6th. Rates, *mann'd with no less than* [1] 1310 Men, *besides* Yachts.

The present want of small Frigates to be supplied by two in each year.

V. Lastly, *In consideration of your* Majesty's *present and growing* Want *of nimble and less chargeable* Frigats, *for answering the ordinary* Occasions *of your* Service, *and which* (*through the general* Age *of your* Old *ones*) *you have already in some degree, and will indispensably be yet more constrain'd to supply, by* Ships *of less* use *and greater* Charge; *you may also expect a* Recruit *of such* Vessels *supply'd you new off of the* Stocks, *by two in each* year.

A Supplemental **Proposition**, Re-lating to your Ships at Sea.

The Ships at Sea to

As to your Ships *at Sea, whose* Repairs *not being included in the precedent* Propo-sition,

[1] *than add.* S. P.

fition, *will neverthelefs (through their* *long continuances abroad) require being* *lookt after, as faft as your* Service will *admit of their being call'd home;* your Majefty *may reafonably depend upon having them alfo put into a full* Repair, *and fupply'd with fix Months* Sea-Stores, *and both them, and the whole* Fleet, (*when once in like manner* repair'd) *kept for ever fo (or made good by* New *ones to be built in their* Rooms, *as they become* irrepairable) *without other* Charge *to* your Majefty, *than what arifes from the* Allowance *ordinarily made for* Wear *and* Tear *during their ftays abroad, rated but at* 22 s. per Man *a* Month, *inftead of the* 30 s. *at which it has ever hitherto been eftimated, and never yet prov'd to have* Coft *the* Crown *fo little.*

be repair- *ed, and* *they and* *the whole* Navy *kept for* *ever fo,* *or new* ones [1] *built, for* 22 s. per *Man a* *Month* *Wear and* *Tear.*

Digefted by the Command, and
 fubmitted with all Humility to
 the Correction of Your Majefty.
       S. Pepys.

[1] ones *add.* S. P.

𝕿𝖍𝖎𝖘

The Proposition approved.

This done, and the *King* with the Lord *Treasurer* upon several *Debates* approving it; His *Majesty* was pleas'd to determine upon an immediate putting the same in *Execution*, by suspending for a time the ordinary *Methods* of his *Navy*, and calling in to his Assistance some other *Hands*, upon whose *Experience* and *Industry* (in conjunction with a *select* Number of the present *Board*) he conceived he might with better security rely for the future success of his *Service: Contented* nevertheless (though[1] from an *Expectation* wholly unsuccessful) to continue the *Remainder* of them (freed of all other *Services*, than that of bringing-up the *Accounts* of their own time, and more particularly of the *Thirty New Ships*) in the same full *Salary* during this *Suspension*, which they before enjoy'd, and was not now to be exceeded even to *Those* on whom was to lie, the *Care* of *Recovering* in *Three* years, what under them had in the *miscarrying* cost the Crown *Five*.

Present Methods of the Navy to be suspended, and new hands entertained.

The old Board nevertheless to be kept in full Salary.

[1] though *add.* S. P.

To=

Towards putting which in prac-   *The New*
tice, the firft ftep was the *Choice* of the   *Hands to*
Hands fo to be entertain'd. Wherein   *be chofen*
(as in the former) His *Majefty* requiring   *by their*
                                              Qualifi-
the fervice of my *Place*, I could not   *cations;*
think of a more proper *Method* of   *and thofe*
difcharging my *Duty* in it, than by   *Qualifi-*
                                         cations
laying before him (for his better   *what.*
diftinguifhing who *were*, from who
were not fit for his Ufe, on an Occafion
fo little able to bear with any miftake
therein) the *Qualifications*, which (as
far as they were attainable) I conceiv'd
ought to be aim'd at, in preference to
all other *Regards*, in this *Election*.
And thefe I accordingly with all fub-
miffion tender'd him, in the Order
and Terms following, *Viz*.

I. *A* Practic'd Knowledge *in every*   *Practiced*
Part of the Works *and* Methods *of your*   *Know-*
Navy, both at the Board *and in your*   *ledge.*
Yards. *The not difcerning of which (and*
the others that follow) appears to have
coft your Royal Brother *and* You *within*
the foremention'd five years, above half a
Million.

                          II. *A*

Account-
antſhip.

    II. A General Maſtery *in the buſineſs of* Accounts, *though more particularly thoſe incident to the Affairs of Your* Navy.

Vigour.

    III. Vigour of Mind, *joyn'd with approv'd* Induſtry, Zeal, *and* Perſonal *aptneſs for* Labour.

Cloſeneſs of Appli-
cation.

    IV. An entire Reſignation *of them-ſelves and their whole time to this Your* Service, *without lyableneſs to* Avocation *from other* Buſineſs *or* Pleaſure.

Credit for
integrity
and Loy-
alty.

    V. Laſtly, ſuch Credit *with your* Majeſty *for* Integrity *and* Loyalty, *as may (with the former conditions) lead both Your* Self *and my Lord* Treaſurer, *to an entire confidence of having all done that can be morally expected from them, in the* Advancement *of your* Service, *and the Circumſpect and Orderly* Diſpen-ſing *and* Improving *of your* Treaſure.

The
Kings
choice.

    Which *Limitations* His *Majeſty* having by a deliberate and diſtinct Application of them to the Nature, Importance, and multiplicity of the *ſervices* to be at the ſame time pain-fully and knowingly attended to in
this

this Affair, he judg'd them of behoof
to be obſerved; and after a moſt
ſolicitous enquiry made, and Collection had of as many Perſons (and
all, God knows, but few) as the Navy
of *England* could furniſh him with,
qualify'd in any competent wiſe to an-
ſwer the Characters beforemention'd,
He was pleas'd to fix his choice upon

Sr. *Anthony Deane.*

Sr. *John Berry.*

Mr. *Hewer.*

Mr. *St. Michel.*

And this with ſo little privity on
their part to ought of His *Majeſties*
Proceedings herein; That could the
King have ſatisfy'd himſelf in the
fitneſs of any one other Perſon within
his *Dominions* for ſupplying his Room,
Sir *Anthony Dean* had prevail'd for *Sir* Ant.
his being excus'd. So inſtant, even Dean's
to Offence (as the then Lord *Treaſurer* *endea-*
will, I perſwade my ſelf, eaſily re- *vour to*
member) were his *Solicitations* to be *avoid it.*
                    ſo;

fo ; as having (befides his being now
fettled in a more beneficial *Courfe* of
Negotiation) induftrioufly flung up
(in the Year 1680) the fame *Charge*
of a *Commiffioner* of the *Navy* ; from

*The
Kings
final in-
fifting on
his Ser-
vice.*
his early profpect of its falling into
that *Condition,* in which His *Majefty*
now found it, and out of which he
was therefore pleas'd finally to infift
upon Sir *Anthony Deane's* return to his
Affiftance in the refcuing it.

*And his
induce-
ment to
the Choice
of him.*
Nor was the *King* led to this fingu-
larity of Opinion in favour of Sir
Anthony Deane, from any lefs inducement, than what arofe from a
deliberate perufal of a Memorial
I had on that Occafion prepar'd for
him, containing a Lift of every Perfon
then occurring to me (whether in or
out of his *Service*) of more than common reckoning among the *Profeffors*
and *Practicers* of *Shipwrightry* within
this Kingdom. Which Memorial I
here fubjoyn, as evidencing more than
enough the *reafonablenefs* (or rather
neceffity) of this his *Majefty's* Choice,
in

in the bare application of the foremention'd conditions (refpectively) to
the Perfons nam'd therein.

March 9. 168$\frac{5}{6}$

A **Memorial** *for the* King *towards
the* Choice *of a Perfon* (*qualify'd
as a* Shipwright) *to supply the want
of* Sir Anthony Deane, *in the*
Commiffion *now prepared for the*
Navy; *the fame feeming Reducible,
To fuch as are in the Service,
either of*

The King, *as his*

	Places.	Persons.	
Commiffio-ners at the }	Navy Board {	S. J. Tippets	A Lift of the moft eminent prefent Ship-wrights of Eng-land.
		S. Phin. Pett	
Mafter Ship-wrights at {	Chatham	Mr. Lee	
	Portfmouth	Mr. Betts	
	Deptford	Mr. J. Shifh	
	Woolwich	Mr. Lawrence	
	Sheernefs	Mr. Furzer	
Mafter Ship-wrights Af-fiftants at {	Chatham {	Mr. Dummer	
		Mr. Pett	
	Portfmouth	Mr. Stiggand	
	Deptford	Mr. Harding	

Or

Or the Merchants, as

	Places.	Perfons.
Private Buil- ders at	Blackwal	Sir *H. Johnson* Mr. *Collins*
	Deptford	Mr. *R. Castle*
	Redr. Ratcl. &c. in the Thames.	Mr. *Graves* Mr. *Jon. Shish* Mr. *Barham* Mr *Narbrow*

By the King's Command,

S. PEPYS.

The general Scheme of the Provision now made of Hands, for the service of the Navy.

And fo the *Provision* made by His *Majesty* for conducting the *whole* of his *Growing* fervices, and adjufting the *Accounts* of thofe *past*, was concerted out of the *Old*, affifted by *New Members*, under the following *Distribution*, Viz.

The

	The whole of the Commiſſion.	For the Growing Services.		For adjuſting the paſt Accounts.
		At the Board.	At the Yards.	
Old	L. *Falkeland* S. *J. Tippets* S. *R. Haddock.* S. *P. Pett* S. *J. Narbrough* Mr. *Southerne* S. *R. Beach* S. *J. Godwin*	L. *Falkeland* S. *J. Narbrough* S. *J. Godwin*	 S. *P. Pett* at *Chatham* S. *R. Beach* at *Portſmouth*	L. *Falkeland* S. *J. Tippets* S. *R. Haddock* Mr. *Southerne*
New	S. *Ant. Deane* S. *J. Berry* Mr. *Hewer* Mr. S. *Michael*	S. *A. Dean* S. *J. Berry* Mr. *Hewer.*	 Mr. St. *Michel* at *Dept. & Woolw.*	

The Lord *Falkeland* remaining
Treaſurer for the Whole.

𝕻𝖚𝖗𝖘𝖚𝖆𝖓𝖙 to this *Scheme*, the *King* by his *Letters Patents* of the 17*th.* of *April* 1686. after declaring that the *Enquiries* he had made ſince his coming to the *Throne* into the *State* of his *Royal Navy*, had diſcover'd it ſuch, as

The Kings Commiſſion purſuant thereto. April 17. 1686.

as call'd for some extraordinary *Appli-cation* for the putting it into that *Condition* of *Force* and *Discipline*, whereto his *Royal* Purpose was to restore and advance it ; and that the weight and diversity of *Works* to be now perform'd, with greater *Vigour* and *Good-Husbandry* than he found to have been for some time [1] exercis'd therein, requir'd a *Distribution* of them answer-able to the different *Qualifications* of the *Persons* he had to intrust with them ; constituted these *Gentlemen* his *Commissioners*, charg'd with the *Duties* assign'd to each in the foregoing *Table*, and the *Instructions* annext to their *Commission*. Among which, to those intrusted with the *growing services*, this was one, *Viz.*

The Workes of the Navy to be better look'd after.

That forasmuch as from the present Disorders under which the whole business of the Office *of his* Navy *was fallen, through the* liberty *for some time taken of committing the most important Parts of it to* Clerks *and inferiour* Instru-ments, *in lieu of the* Officers *themselves*

These Commis-sioners made equally account-able for the whole.

[1] sometime *corr.* S. P.

per-

perſonally charg'd therewith, He had *(anſwerable to what was ſucceſsfully done* by His Royal Grand-father, *King* James, *on a like Occaſion) thought it neceſſary to put the ſame in to* Commiſſion, *until the ancient* Order *and* Diſcipline *of it being recover'd, he might with ſafety reſtore it to its former* Method *of* Inſtitution; *He declares His Royal* Intention *and* Expectation *to be, that theſe his* Commiſſioners *hold themſelves* jointly accountable *for the well performance of the* whole, *and ſtand* equally *chargeable with the* Failures *found therein.*

And ſo they enter'd upon the Execution of this *Commiſſion,* as from *Lady-Day* 1686; directing their firſt ſtep to the finding out the true Source of this *ſo unexampled Evil* they were now to contend with, in the moſt tender Part of their Charge, namely, the *New Ships.* Than which as nothing could be more deſerving their niceſt ſearch, with regard to the publick import of the ſubject of it. So neither could any thing be of more

The Commiſſion to operate from Lady Day. 1686.

Enquiry into the trueCauſe of the New Ships *decays.*

particular moment to them, whom the King had thus intrufted with the *Cure*, than an explicite Knowledge of the *Origine* of the *Difeafe*.

Taking therefore this for the proper place of doing it, I here infert a fhort Account of the iffue of thofe *enquiries* of thefe Gentlemen thereinto; and the rather, for the fake of the *unaccountablenefs* of their *Suggeftions*, who would have it wholly imputable to the *Haftinefs* of the *Building*, the *Greennefs* of the *Stuff*, and efpecial *Effects* of the *Eaft-Country-Timber* and *Plank* wrought thereon.

To the two former of which, it was made appear to His *Majefty*, that the *Ship* the *quickeft* built of the whole number lay full *nine* months upon the Stocks, and but *feven* of the thirty lefs than an entire *Year*. Whereas diverfe Inftances were produc'd out of his *Old Navy*, where the *Timber* had been ftanding, cut, and converted, and the *Ships* built therewith, and launched in *fix months*; without having one
Plank

Vulgar fuggeftions toucking the fame.

Haftinefs in Building and Greennefs of Stuff, not chargeable therewith.

Plank shifted in them (but for *Shot*)
in *Eight* or *Nine Years* after.   While
on the contrary, *three* and *twenty* of
these *Thirty* lay from *one* to full *two*,
three, and *four Years* in building, and
the last of them more than *five*; till
above *one hundred pounds* was demanded
by her *Builder* for repairing the Decays
of her very *Keel*, as she lay upon the
Stocks.

And for what concerns the Use of *Nor the*
East-Country-Stuff; it was no less also *use of*
shewn to the *King*, that several *Ships* *East-*
were then subsisting in his *Navy*, *Country-*
planked with no other, which after *Stuff.*
the same Service of *eight* or *nine Years*,
were by many degrees in better *Con-*
dition, than most of these at *three*.

It was moreover observ'd, that not *Forreign*
above *Five* hundred of *Five* and *Thirty* *Timber*
Thousand Loads of *Timber*, provided *little.*
for these Ships, were of *East-Country-*
Growth.

And that for *Plank*; had the *Officers* *Forreign*
of the *Navy* (after twenty years currant *Plank,*
use of it) met with any present Ground *not want-*
                                        ing, in

for fufpecting it, there had been *Englifh* enough (and of proper *Thickneffes*) contracted and paid for by the *King,* for anfwering all the Occafions of their *Buttocks* and *Hoodings* from the *Water's Edge* to their *Gun-deck-Ports* (where this *Evil* was obferv'd principally to feize them) without reforting to the ufe of one Inch of *Eaft-Country.*

The *Mafter-Builders* too, unanimoufly afferted the good Condition of all the *Timber* and *Plank* (whether *Englifh* or *Forreign*) us'd on this Work, equal to the beft they had ever known in the *Navy:* Befides the univerfality of the Practice of all the *Northern Nations,* and not them only, but the *Dutch, French,* and (for feveral years paft) our *own Merchant Builders* too, in the ufe of this *Commodity.* Nor (in a word) did any one Ship appear, among the whole *Thirty,* more complaining, than fome of them, upon which not one Foot of *Eaftland-Plank* or *Timber* had been wrought.

All

All which notwithſtanding; ſuch did theſe *Gentlemen* eſteem the Weight of this *Cauſe*, with reſpect no leſs to the *fatality* on one hand attending the uſe of this *Commodity* upon theſe Ships, in caſe the ſame ſhould be found truely *faulty*; than on the other, to the conſequences of the *Miſtake*, ſhould it indeed prove otherwiſe, at a ſeaſon, wherein the *ſervice* of it was become next to indiſpenſable, for the preſent Repair of the *Fleet*; That their *Commiſſion* was no ſooner opened, but a ſolemn *Conference* was held by them with all the Eminent *Maſter Builders* in the River of *Thames*, upon this *Subject*. The *Iſſue* of which having been preſented to the *King*, he was pleas'd to make it ſo much a matter of *State*, as to command my bringing it ſome time after to the *Council-Table*. Of whoſe *Reſolution* thereon, and the reſult of the foregoing *Conference*, I have ſubjoyn'd Copies, as of a *Matter* moſt worthy the Notice of every *Engliſh Gentleman*,
tho

Import-
ance of
a right
determin-
ation in
this mat-
ter.

A ſolemn
Confere-
ence with
the moſt
eminent
Mr. Ship-
wrights
of Eng-
land
about it.

tho more particularly thofe, who are converfant in the *Timber-Trade* of this Kingdom.

RESOLUTIONS,

Taken at a Conference *held at the* Office *of the* Navy, *April.* 17. 1686. *between His Majefty's* Commiffioners *there, and us the under-written* Ship-wrights, *upon* Enquiries *then propos'd by the* Secretary *of the* Admiralty *on behalf of His* Majefty, *touching the prefent* Condition *of this* Kingdom, *in reference to* 𝕻𝖑𝖆𝖓𝖐 *for* Ship-Building.

Enquiry I.

How far it may be depended on, that England *may at this day fupply it felf with a fufficiency of that* Commodity, *for anfwering the Occafions both of the* Merchants *and His* Majefty's *fervice (in the State the* Royal Navy *thereof now is) without* Foreign *Help?*

Refo-

Resolution.

That it is in no wise to be rely'd *Plank not* on. Forasmuch as from the want *sufficient* of *Plank* of our *own Growth*, and *of English* consequently the highness of *Price* *answer* of what we have ; the *Shipwrights* of *all the* this Kingdom (even in our *Out-Ports*, *present* as well as in the River of *Thames*) *for the* have been for many years past, driven *same.* to resort to supplys *from Abroad*[1], and are so at this day, to the Occasioning their spending of *One Hundred* Loads of *Forreign*, for every *Twenty* of *English*. Besides, were our *own* Stock more ; the exclusion of *Forreign* Goods would soon render the Charge of Building *insupportable*, by raising the *Price* of the Commodity to double what it is, and more, at the pleasure of the *Seller*.

Enquiry II.

From whence is the best Forreign Plank *understood to be brought?*

[1] *Aboard corr.* S. P.   *Reso-*

Resolution.

*Best for-
reign
Plank
from
whence.*

Either out of the *East-Sea* from
Dantzick, *Quinborow*, or *Riga* of the
Growth of *Poland* and *Prussia*, or from
Hambrough, namely, that sort thereof,
which is Shipt from thence of the
Growth of *Bohemia*, distinguished by
its Colour, as being much more black
than the other, and rendred so (as is
said) by its long sobbing in the water,
during its Passage thither.

Enquiry III.

What Proportion *this* Forrein Plank
may be reckoned to bear to the English,
with regard to its Use, Cost, *and*
Durableness?

Resolution.

*The Use,
Cost, and
Durable-
ness of
forreign
Plank
compared
with
English.*

For so much as concerns *smaller
Vessels* of Fourscore Tuns downwards
(whose works call not for more than
2 Inch Plank, of 20 Foot long at the
highest, meeting at 13 and 14 Inches
in breadth) our *English* Plank will
(from

(from the Nature of the Wood) laſt
longer than any *Forreign* of the ſame
Dimenſions. But for *Ships* of 300
Tuns upwards, which require the ſervice of 3 and 4 Inch-Plank from 26
to 40 Foot long, meeting at 14 or
15 Inches breadth at the Top-end;
Univerſal practice ſhews, that the
White Crown-*Plank* of *Pruſſia*, and
the fore-mentioned *Black* of *Bohemia*,
do in their durableneſs equal or
rather exceed that of Our *Engliſh*
Production of like Dimenſions.

Which we conceive to ariſe from
this plain Reaſon, *viz.* That the
Forreign Oak being of much quicker
growth than ours, their Trees arrive
at a Stature capable of yielding *Plank*
of theſe *Meaſures*, while they are yet
in their ſound and vigorous *State* of
growing; whereas that of *England*
advancing in its Growth more ſlowly,
arrives not at theſe Dimenſions, till
it be come to or rather is paſt the
full of its *Strength*; fifty *Years* ſufficing
for raiſing the *Forreign*, to what the

*Conject-
ure at the
Phyſical
reaſon of
the differ-
ent dura-
bleneſs
of for-
reign and
Engliſh
Plank of
the larger
Dimen-
ſions.*

Eng-

English will not be brought in an hundred and fifty.

But whether we are right or not in this Reaſoning, it is upon daily experience moſt evident; that our *Eaſt-India*, and other *Ships* of greateſt *Burthen*, built with this large *Forreign* Plank, well choſen, prove in their *Durableneſs* without exception; variety of Inſtances lying before us, of *Ships* built wholy with *English* ſtuff, (as well in His *Majeſties* Yards as *Merchants*) which have periſh'd in half the time, others of like Burthen, compos'd wholly of *Forreign*, have been obſerv'd to do.

From hence alſo it is, that though *English Plank* of *Short* Lengths, cut out of young *Growing* Timber, is manifeſtly better than *Eaſt-Country*, and therefore is preferred thereto in laying of a *Gun-Deck*, as far as the three ſtreaks next the Ships ſides, where ſhort ſtuff will ſerve (the *Quality* of its *Wood* bearing better with being kept *Wet* and *Dry*, as it generally is
in

in that place. Yet where (upon the
fame *Gun-deck*) *long Plank* is neceſſary,
that of *Forreign* growth is for Strength
and duration always preferr'd, from
the reaſon (as we conceive) before
given, namely, of its being cut while
in its *Vigour*, which the *Engliſh* will not
admit, ſo as to bear thoſe *Scantlings*.

And to this is to be further added,
the general *Wanineſs*, want of *Breadth*
at the *Top-end*, and ill method of
Converſion of our *Engliſh* Plank; daily
practice ſhewing, that twenty Loads
of *Forreign* ſhall in working go further
upon a Ships ſide or Deck, than
a hundred *Loads* of like Lengths of
Engliſh, after its *Wanes* and other
Defects ſhall be cut away.

Moreover it is yet to be noted,
that in planking of a Ship with
Forreign Plank, the Builder ſhall not
be driven to put in above three or
four Pieces, where in a like Ship done
with *Engliſh*, he ſhall be obliged to
uſe a hundred; to the no leſs impair-
ment of the *ſtrength* of the Work,
than

*General
wanineſs,
want of
Breadth
at the
Top end,
and ill
Conver-
ſion of
Engliſh
Plank.*

*Encreaſe
of Work
and
Charge
ariſing
there-
from.*

than increase of its *Charge*, both in Stuff and Labour.

So that upon the whole, our unanimous *Opinion* is ; that large *Plank*, well chosen, of the *Forreign* growths beforemention'd, is in its service at least as *durable*, in its cost less *Chargeable*, and the use of it (through the scarcity of *English*) become at this day *indispensable*.

Jonas Shish.	*Hen. Johnson.*
Pet. Norberry.	*Abra. Greaves.*
Jos. Lawrence.	*John Shish.*
Ja. Yeames.	*Wil. Collins.*
Rob. Castel.	

By *the* Commissioners *of the* NAVY.

We do fully concur in the *Resolutions* above-written.

A. Deane.
J. Narbrough.
J. Berry.
Ph. Pet.
Wil. Hewer.
B. S. Michel.

Mem=

Samuel Pepys, an oil painting by Sir Godfrey Kneller completed in 1689
at around the time Pepys was working on his *Memoires of the Royal Navy*.
(National Maritime Museum BHC2947)

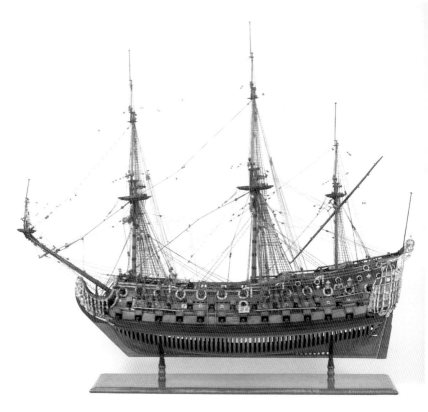

A seventeenth-century model of the *Coronation*, the last Second Rate of the 1677
'thirty ships' programme to be completed, in 1685. The condition of two
of her sister-ships, the *Vanguard* and *Ossory*, became a matter
of considerable controversy. (Kriegstein Collection)

Two Third Rates, the backbone of the battlefleet in the age of sail, depicted in exquisite drawings by Willem van de Velde the elder. The *Harwich* (above) was designed by Anthony Deane, a close associate of Pepys and probably the Kings's favourite shipbuilder. The *Lenox* (below) was built a few years later and was the first Third Rate of the 1677 programme to be completed. Shown here when laid up in the 1680s, the neglect of these new ships in this period became a matter of political scandal. (National Maritime Museum PY9360 and PT2427)

A royal visit to the fleet in 1672. The centre of attention
is the 100-gun *Prince*, the flagship of the Duke of York,
later King James II, a man who became Pepys' most influential patron.

The royal yachts, seen to the left, were one manifestation of the love of the navy demonstrated by both Charles and James, an affection signally lacking in William III. (National Maritime Museum BHC0299)

Details of the stern carvings, with the prominent Stuart arms on the taffrail, of the Third Rate *Monck* of 1660. A relatively old ship, she is shown as under repair in Pepys' 1688 list but was to serve until 1702 before being completely rebuilt. (National Maritime Museum PZ7275)

Marginally more numerous than Third Rates in the fleet, Fourth Rates were general-purpose ships, capable of fighting in major battles but equally useful for cruising independently or escorting convoys. No other ship of this rate was as elaborately decorated as the *Woolwich* shown in this oil painting, but most were similar in size and layout. (National Maritime Museum BHC3732)

The old Fifth Rate *Dartmouth* of 1655 was listed by Pepys as a fireship, and was indeed one of many hasty conversions undertaken in 1688 in the face of the threat from William's Dutch fleet. After the 'Glorious Revolution' she reverted to a cruising warship and made her name at the relief of Londonderry the following year. (National Maritime Museum PY3907)

The Sixth Rate *Drake*, 14 guns, was one of the smallest regular warships of the Pepysian era. Built in 1651, the ship was still a nominal member of the fleet at the time Pepys wrote but was in Jamaica where she was about to be condemned as beyond repair and sold. (National Maritime Museum PY1876)

𝕸𝖊𝖒𝖔𝖗𝖆𝖓𝖉𝖚𝖒, That thefe *Refolu-tions* from the Body of the *Mafter Builders* of *England,* confirm'd by the *Commiffioners* of the *Navy,* to my Enquiries touching *Foreign* Plank, were Communicated by me to His *Majefty* (my Lord *Treafurer* prefent) *October* the 7*th.* and by His fpecial Command prefented to Him again (with a Memorial attending it) at the *Council Table,* Oct. 8*th.* 1686. *Prefentation thereof to the King and from him to the Council-Board.*

S. PEPYS.

At the Court *at* Whitehall
Oct. 8. 1686.

PRESENT

The *Kings* moft Excellent *Majefty.*

His R. H. Pr. *George* of *Denmark,* &c.

A Paper *having been this day* (*by his* Majefties *command*) *prefented to the* Board *by Mr.* Pepys *Secretary of the* Admiralty *of* England, *containing certain* Refolutions *taken at a* Conference *held at the Office of the Navy the* 17. *of* April *Order of Council in approval and confirmation of the foregoing Report.*

April *laſt, between his Majeſties* Commiſſioners *there, and the Body of the
moſt eminent* Ship-Builders *of this
Kingdom, upon* Enquiries *propoſed to
them by the ſaid* Secretary *on behalf and
by direction of his* Majeſty, *touching
the preſent condition of* England *in
reference to* Plank *for Ship-building,
and the ſaid* Paper *being now read and
ſolemnly conſider'd*; *His* Majeſty *was
pleaſed to declare his being ſo far convinc'd there-from of the* ſafety, benefit,
and preſent neceſſity *of making uſe of*
Plank *of* Foreign *growth in the Building
and Repairing of His* Royal Navy, *as
to reſolve*; *That the* Principal Officers
and Commiſſioners *of his* Navy *be at
liberty to contract for and make uſe in
his Services aforeſaid of* Oaken Plank
of Foreign *growth, of the Sorts mention'd
in the* Reſolution *to the Second Enquiry
contain'd in the ſaid* Paper; *and to
Order, that the ſaid* Original Paper
under the Hands of the Commiſſioners
of the Navy *and* Maſter Builders, *be
(for the* publick Importance *thereof)*
                                        care-

carefully laid up and preferv'd among the Papers and Records of the Council-Table.

John Nicholas.

𝕿𝖍𝖊 prefent *Effects* of which laft Papers and the *Obfervations* next preceding, amounting to nothing lefs than a plain *Detection* of the *Vanity* of thofe *fuggeftions* touching the Root of this *Calamity*; Nought remain'd whereon the fame could with any appearance of *Confequence* be charg'd, fave the plain *Omiffion* of the neceffary and ordinary *Cautions* us'd for the preferving of *New-built Ships*. Divers of them appearing not to have been once *Grav'd* nor brought into *Dock*, fince they were Launched. Others that had been *Dockt*, fent out again in a *Condition* needing to be brought-in a fecond time. Their *Holds* not clean'd nor air'd, but (for want of *Gratings* and opening their *Hatches* and *Scuttles*) fuffer'd to heat and moulder, till I have with my own Hands gather'd *Toad-ftools* growing

The true Grounds of the New-Ships Decays.

Want of Graving & bringing into Dock.

Holds not clean'd nor ayr'd. Gratings wanting. Hatches and Scuttles not opened.

Not heel'd or breemed.

Expofed to the Sun, with their Sides unwatered.

Not Ballafted enough to deepen them in the Water.

Ports not opened in dry weather.

Scuppers wanting on the Gundecks, in wet.

Planks not opened upon the firft difcovery

in the moft confiderable of them, as big as my *Fifts*. Some not once *heel'd* or *breem'd* fince their building, but expos'd in hot weather to the *Sun*, broiling in their *Buttocks* and elfewhere, for want of cooling with *Water* (according to the Practice of our own, as well as all *Forreign* Nations) and that *Expofure* yet magnifi'd, by their want of *Ballaft* for bringing them deep enough into the *Water*. *Port-Ropes* alfo wanting wherewith to open the *Ports*, for airing them in *Dry* weather; and *Scuppers* upon their *Gun-decks* in *Wet*, to prevent the finking of *Rain* through their fhrunken *Seams* into their *Holds* and among their *Timbers*. *Planks* not open'd upon the firft Difcovery of their *Decays*, nor *Pieces* put in, where defective; but inftead thereof, repair'd only with *Caps* of *Board*[1] and *Canvas*. Which ought alfo to have been done upon the *Ordinary Eftimate* of the *Navy*, that provides for every thing needful to the *Prefervation* of Ships in *Harbour*, but

[1] *Boards corr.* S. P.

but more especially for the Graving *of their* one *Third* of the whole every *Year*; *Decays,* whereas some (even of the *Old Ships*) *nor those* appear not to have been so look'd *duely* after, in five or six. *looked to.*

From which, and other like *Omis-* *The effect* *sions*, it could not but fall out (as *of these* indeed it did) that some of these un- *Omissions* fortunate *Ships* were already become *observ'd.* rotten, while others built of the very same *Stuff*, at the *same Place*, by the same *Hand*, and within the very *same Time* for *Merchant-service*, suc⟨c⟩eeded well and continu'd so.

And with the *Navy* thus disorder'd, *The En-* these *Gentlemen* (as I have said) enter'd *try and* upon their *Commission*. And with what *¹procedure* Spirit and under what View they pro- *of* ¹ *these* ceeded thereon, will be best Collected *Commis-* from their own *Annual Reports* thereof *sioners.* to the *King*, consonant (through the whole) to the few following Para- graphs, *viz.*

August 1687.

We tender in all humility to Your

Ma-

Majefty *our humble* Reprefentation *of the* Effects *of that* Commiffion, *to which you were pleas'd to call us*; *and*

With Sin- *which we have endeavour'd to performe*
cerity and *with a fincerity and plainnefs, anfwerable*
plainnefs. (*as far as we are able*) *to the extra-*
Called by *ordinarinefs of that Favour, wherewith*
the King (*without our* expectation) *we were called*
without
their ex- *thereto———*
pectation.

Graving *Whereas among other the Works of your*
and or- Navy, *that of* Graving *and well perform-*
dinary *ing the* Ordinary *Repairs of your Ships in*
Repairs. Harbour, *holds a principal Place. As that, to the want of which, a great* (*if not the greateft*) *fhare of the* Calamity *whereinto they* (*and particular⟨l⟩y the* Thirty New Ones) *have been fuffer'd to fall, is moft rightfully to be imputed*; *and has therefore the firft place given* [1] *it by your* Majefty *in this* propofition. *We have moft diligently apply'd our felves to an effectual anfwering every* part *thereof* (*both as to* Works *and* payments)

The De- *as far at leaft as the* Defects *of the faid*
cays long *Ships, fo long in* Arrear, *could within this*
in arrear. *time be difcover'd and purfu'd———*

[1] giving; *corr.* S. P.

When

When it shall be consider'd, how deeply *the Ships were infected with that* evil, *by which they were (even in their* Thickeft ftuff*) become* rotten *and reduc'd to* powder. *It seems a matter of too great presumption (without wholly stripping them) to* undertake *against any possible* remains *or* returns *of the said* evil. *But this we take Liberty to say*————

And however more or less successful our Managements *may be found to be in the well husbanding of your* Treasure *herein; We are not conscious of being able to mend it, were we to* Act *the same over again, and the* Gain *or* Loss *arising therefrom to* affect *our* own *Purses, as they now do* Your *Majesty's.*

And their infection too deep, for any undertaking of their cure without wholly striping them.

Good Husbandry herein asserted.

Falkeland.	J. Godwin.
A. Deane.	Ph. Pett.
J. Narbrough.	W. Hewer.
J. Berry.	B. St. Michel.

𝕬𝖚𝖌𝖚𝖘𝖙 1688.

Though we need no greater Affurance, *than what* Your *Majefty has already on every Occafion given us, of Your Gracious*

Opinion

Opinion of our *Humble* Endeavours *in this Your Service. Yet cannot we forbear*

The effects of their Service greater, had not the Works proved worse than estimated.

observing to *Your Majesty, that the* Effects *thereof might have prov'd greater (though our* Industry *could not) had not the State of Your* Ships *prov'd much worse, and by consequence the* Work *and* Charge *of them weightier, than they were Estimated in the Surveys and Calculations, upon which that* Proposition *was founded, and the Execution of it committed to us; besides the difficulties we have had to*

Obstructions industriously offered them and whence.

contend with, *from* Obstructions *and* Hardships *industriously put upon us (both from* Sea *and* Shore) *by those to whom our Methods of* Good Husbandry *and* Dispatch *proved less grateful, than the* Laxeness *in both, to which they had for some time been accustom'd*—————

The well performance of the Works.

As to the complete Performance *of these* Works, *as far as Matters of this kind can be judg'd of, and in a Case so extraordinary as that of the* State *whereinto Your* Royal Navy *was fallen at the time of your calling us to the remedying it; We have not only our own* Observations,

tions, *and the ampleness of those our*
Orders *by which the said* Works *were directed to be performed; but the* Reports
of your Master-Builders *charg'd with
the conducting them, confirm'd by your*
Commissioners *of the* Yards *where they
were severally perform'd. Beyond which
we cannot conceive any thing capable of*
being added towards the satisfying either
Your Majesty, *or our selves therein. And
though we do not believe so much to have
been ever before shewn in the Case of
a like* Fleet. *Yet, regard being had to
what* Experience *dayly informs us, of*
the Defects *discover'd upon ransacking
of their* Seams *by the* Caulkers, *we dare
not mislead your* Majesty *to think, that
(after so general and deep a* Decay, *as
this* Fleet *was fallen into, before any
fitting* Application *was made for its*
Remedy) *all the Care that has been
taken in the shifting of its* Timbers
and Plank *(as far as any Defects have
appear'd) can upon fresh* Ransacking,
secure your Majesty *against the appearance
of further* Remains, *till the first* Materials
about

about the Breadths *and adjacent* Parts
(*especially of the* New Ships) *shall by
degrees be entirely remov'd* ————

The Ships yet to be finished for compleating the Proposition.

It rests to give Your Majesty *the*
Names *of your* Ships *under present*
Repair, *and those remaining to be
repair'd when they shall be finish'd for
compleating your whole* Navy, *according
to* Mr. Pepys's *Proposition,* Viz.

Ships under Repair.		Remaining to be Repair'd.	
Ships,	Yard.	Ships,	Yard.
St. *Michael* Roy. *Kathe-rine* *Brittannia*	} *Chath.*	*Prince* *Victory* *Royal Oak*	} *Chath.*
St. *George* *Monck*	} *Portsm.*	*King-Fi-sher*	} *Deptf.*
Happy Re-turn *Oxford*	} *Woolw.*		
Portland *Phænix*	} *Deptf.*		

Falkeland.   Ph. Pett.
A. Deane.   W. Booth.
J. Berry.   W. Hewer.
B. S. Michel.

$\mathfrak{This}$

This while in doing, towards the *Discipline to be recovered and Disorders reformed at Sea.* Amendment of matters on *Shore*, and the *State* of the *Ships* in *Harbour*; no less thoughtfulness was at work for the *Recovery* of good *Discipline* and *Reformation* of *Disorders* at *Sea*. And this pursu'd, to the drawing a no *And not without charge to the Crown, for the better satisfaction of Commanders, &c.* inconsiderable *Encrease* of standing *Charge* upon the *Crown*, the more surely to effect his Majesties desires herein, with the *satisfaction* of his *Commanders* and other his *Officers* and *Seamen* interested in the same. The evidencing of which will not need more than one of sundry instances to be produc'd of it, namely, that of the *Establishment* *Instanced in the Establishment about Captains Tables, Forreign Prizes, &c.* in *July* 1686. (of near *Date* with the foregoing *Commission*) the Tenor whereof follows.

His Majesties Regulation in the business of Plate-Carriage, &c. *with his Establishment of an Allowance to his* Sea-Commanders *for their* Tables *and other* Encouragements *to them, their* Officers, *and* Companies.

James

James R.

'WHereas from the *Enquiries* by
us folemnly made (fince our
acceffion to the *Throne* of this our
Kingdom of *England*) into the [1] *State*
of our *Royal Navy*, and the general

Diforders in the Navy enquired into, by the King. *Diforders* into which both it and its
Difcipline have of late years fallen,
we are (among the many other *Evils*
difcovered therein, and which we
have already in great meafure provided *Remedies* to) arrived at a full
Information in that particular one,
whereto our Service is in a moft
efpecial manner expofed, from the
liberty taken by *Commanders* of our
Ships (upon all opportunities of private profit) of converting the Service

Particularly the diverting the publick fervice of his Ships to private ufes. of our faid Ships to their own ufe,
and the total neglect of the *Publick*
Ends for which they, at our great
Charge, are fet forth and maintained,
namely, the annoying of our *Enemies*,
the protecting the Eftates of our
Trading-Subjects, and the fupport of

[1] the *repeated in ed.*; *corr.* S. P.

our

our honour with *Forreign Princes.* And
forasmuch also as this *Evil* seems
principally to arise from the universal
abuse of the liberty for some time
indulged to Our said *Commanders,*
of Transporting of *Plate, Bullion,* and
Jewels; to the occasioning thereby
the said General mis-employment of
our *Ships,* and our want of those full
and frequent *Accounts* of the *Proceedings* of our Commanders abroad, which
by their known *Instructions* they stand
obliged to give us. Our *Will* and
pleasure is, and it is hereby solemnly
declared.

Arising from the abused liberty of carrying Plate, &c.

' I. That no *Admiral, Commander in
Chief, Captain* of any of our *Ships,* or
other *Officers* serving us therein, shall
presume from henceforward upon any
pretence, or by vertue of any former
Allowance, Instruction, or Practice
whatsoever, to receive direct, or permit to be received, on board any of
our said Ships, any *Mony, Plate, Bullion, Jewels,* or other *Merchandize* or
Goods (fine or gross) whatsoever, whether
be-

Plate carriage, &c. restrained.

belonging to Strangers or our own
Subjects, either under pretext of con-
cealing or protecting the same, or
the Transporting thereof from Port
to Port, or from any Forreign Port
for *England,* whether upon *Application*
to them made by any our *Merchant-
Subjects* in Forreign parts, or from
any other inducement whatsoever,
saving by Written Warrant under
our own *Royal* hand, and that only ;
upon pain of being (on conviction)
immediately discharged from their
present, and rendred incapable of
any future Employment in our Service ; as also of refunding to the
use of our *maimed* Seamen of the
Chest at *Chatham,* the full value of
the profits they shall be found to
have made by any violation of this
our Order, and of suffering such further punishment, as by the *Laws* of
the *Sea,* they shall become liable to
for the same.

' II. That none of our aforesaid
General Officers or private *Commanders*
shall

shall, (upon like forfeiture and pen- *The like* alties) prefume to carry, or direct *as to* the carrying any *Paſſenger* or *Paſ-* *carrying* *fengers* (whether ſtrangers or others) *of Paſ-* of what Degree or Quality ſoever, *fengers.* from one place to another, in any of our *Ships* of *War* under their Command, unleſs by like particular Order given in Writing from our felf for their ſo doing; ſuch only excepted, as by the Eleventh Article *With Ex-* of our preſent General *Inſtructions* *ceptions.* they are obliged to receive and give paſſage to; namely, our *Subjects* redeemed from *Slavery, Shipwreckt,* or taken at Sea out of *Forreign* Ships.

'III. That all *Admirals* and *Com-* *Copies of* *manders in Chief* of Our Ships do for *all Sail-* the time to come take care, that as *ders iſſued* often as they ſhall have occaſion of *or receiv-* giving *Orders* for the proceeding of *ed at Sea* any of Our *Ships* under their Com- *to be* mand on any Service, the ſame be *ted to the* done in Writing under their hands, *Secretary* with *Copies* thereof to be ſent by the *of the* *Admir-* firſt *alty.*

firſt opportunities of conveyance (by Land and Sea) to the *Secretary* of our *Admiralty* for our information. And that the ſame be in like manner done by the *Commanders* of every of our *private* Ships, in Tranſmitting to our ſaid *Secretary* for our like Information, *Copies* of every *Order* they ſhall receive from their Admiral, Commander in chief, or other Superiour Officer.

The like as to Advices of the Kings Ships coming into forreign Ports, and Abſtraƈts of their Journals.

'IV. That every of our fore-mentioned *Officers* and *Commanders* reſpectively, do obſerve, that as often as our Service requires their going into any *Forreign Port*, they do by the firſt *Poſt* after their arrival, (and ſo from *Poſt* to *Poſt* during their ſtay there) give us (through the hand of our ſaid *Secretary*) a particular Account of their *Proceedings*, from the date of their laſt, with *Abſtracts* of their *Journals* during that time; and that care be taken for their leaving the like with our *Conſul* or other publick *Miniſter* in that Place, to be by him for-

forwarded to our faid *Secretary*, by
the firft Conveyance after their departure thence; fo as we may at all
times have a conftant and thorough
knowledge of the *Condition*, *Services*,
and *Proceedings* of all and every of
our *Ships* employed on Forreign Service, with the occafions of the fame.

Laftly, That at the end of each *The like*
Voyage, an entire *Book* containing *at the*
end of the
a perfect *Journal* thereof, together *Voyage*,
with a *Book* of *Entries* to be kept of *as to their*
all *Orders*, either iffued or received *Journals*,
(as before) by them therein, be de- *and En-*
try-Books
livered for our ufe to our faid *Secre-* *of Orders.*
tary of the *Admiralty* (and fworn to
if required) by every of our faid
Admirals, *Commanders* in *Chief*, and
private *Commanders*, immediately upon
their coming into Port to be laid up,
and before the paying off of the
Ships whereto they refpectively be-
long. Both which *Books* our faid
Secretary is to caufe to be well examined by himfelf, or fuch other
Perfon as fhall be exprefly appointed
                              thereto,

thereto, in order to a *Report* to be therefrom made to us, of the different Degrees of *care* or *neglect* wherewith thefe and all other our *Orders* fhall appear to have been obferved, and our receiving full fatisfaction from them therein, before the payment of their *Wages*, or the further *Allowance* hereafter appointed in confideration of their good Service during their faid *Voyage*.

Univer-fal Ob-fervation of thefe Rules in-joyn'd.

'Of all which as well every our faid *Admirals, Commanders* in *Chief*, private *Commanders* of our *Ships*, and other the Officers within mentioned, as our prefent *Secretary* of our *Admiralty*, and the *Secretary* of our *Admiralty* for the time being, are hereby required to yield full and conftant obedience and conformity, as they will anfwer the contrary at their perils.

And en-couraged by the Eftablifh-ment of an extra-

And to the end, that with the Provifion thus made towards the recovery and advancement of the *Honour, Difcipline,* and *Profperity* of our *Naval-Service,*

Service, We may at the fame time *ordinary allowance to Commanders for fupport of their Tables.* Teftifie our like *Royal* Inclination to the giving all reafonable *Encourage-ment* to thofe, who fhall from hence-forward be employed as *Commanders* in any of our *Ships*; thereby as well to excite and oblige them to a ftrict complyance with thefe and all other our *Royal* Refolutions and Orders, as the better to enable them to fupport the *Charge* and *Dignity* of their faid *Employments* and *Entertainment* therein, without reforting to *Methods* of doing it fo injurious to our *Honour* and *Service,* and wafteful of our *Treafure,* as thofe before-mentioned have been.

'We are in the firft place gracioufly pleafed (in favour to our faid *Commanders*) to take upon our felf an encreafe of *Charge,* beyond what has ever hitherto been at any one time done by any of our *Royal* Predeceffors, namely, by granting (as we hereby do) to the *Commanders* of every of our *Ships* and *Veffels* (*Yachts* only ex-cepted) an annual *Allowance* (over and above

above the value of the *Victualling* they now enjoy in common with their Ship's Companies) for the fupport of their *Tables*, proportioned to the refpective Rates of the Ships and Veffels they fhall happen feverally to Command. The faid *Allowance* to commence upon thofe of our Ships which are now fitting forth, and fhall at any time hereafter be fitted forth to the *Seas*, from the Date and Delivery of their Commanders and Signing Officers joynt *Certificates* to the *Secretary* of our *Admiralty*, and *Commiffioners* of our Navy, of their Ships being compleatly fitted for the Sea, and in readinefs to Execute our final Orders for their Sailing. And upon fuch of our *Ships* as are at this prefent abroad; from the day of their Commanders receiving from our faid *Secretary* (which he is with all convenient fpeed to difpatch to them) Copies of this our Order; and to be continued both on the one and the other to the Determination of their refpective *Voyages*.

‘ The

This Allowance to begin, when.

' The value of which allowance
hereby fo granted is as follows.

A Table of the Annual Allowance of a Sea-Commander of each Rate.									
Rate	Prefent Wages.			Prefent Victualling.			Additional Grant for his Table.		
	£	s.	d.	£	s.	d.	£	s.	d.
I	273	15	0	12	3	4	250	0	0
2	219	00	0	12	3	4	200	0	0
3	182	00	0	12	3	4	166	5	0
4	136	10	0	12	3	4	124	5	0
5	109	10	0	12	3	4	100	0	0
6	91	00	0	12	3	4	83	0	0

The value of that allowance.

'Wherein our *Royal Intention* is, that
this *allowance* for *Tables* granted to
our faid *Commanders* as Captains of
Private Ships, fhall not be conftrued
to the taking away or diminifhing
ought of what has been heretofore
Eftablifhed to *Flag-Officers*, upon Account of their *Flags.*

Without leffening the allowance already eftablifhed to Flags.[1]

'And that we may yet the more
effectually excite to a vigorous profe-

[1] *Flags*] *Fags in ed. corr.* S. P.

cution

A further Grant, to them, their Officers, and Companies, of the whole value of the Prizes taken from the People of Barbary. cution of our *Service,* such of our said *Commanders* as shall be by us employed in our Wars with any of the people of *Barbary,* (such as that wherein we now are, and have, to the great Expence of our *Treasure* and hazard to our *Subjects* Trading into those Seas, for several years been engaged with those of *Sally*) we are graciously pleas'd farther to grant to such our *Commanders,* the full benefit of all Prizes, (both *Hulls, Furniture, Lading* and *Slaves*) that shall be by them taken, whether of *Ships* of *War,* or *Merchant Men*; saving only the Vessels of our *Subjects* happening to have fallen into the hands of such our *Enemies.* In which case, the *Salvage* only of the Vessels of our Subjects so rescued, shall go to the *Retakers.*

'The whole of which forementioned *Prizes* and *Salvage* shall be divided between the *Commander* or *Commanders,* of such our Ship or Ships (with their *Officers* and *Companies*) as were con-

cerned

cerned in the Chafe and *Capture* of
the faid Prizes, according to the *Law*
and *practice* of the *Sea*.

'Provided always, that no part of *Condi-*
the *Charge* of fecuring or maintaining *tions of*
any of the Veffels, Lading, or Com- *lowance.*
panies of the faid *Prizes*, fhall be
placed to our Account, from the day
wherein the fame fhall be firft brought
into any *Chriftian* Port; and that the
faid *Prizes* be carried into Port, with
as little Charge as may be to us, and
without any interruption to the *fervice*
wherein our faid Ships were imployed
at the time of the *Capture*.

'Laftly, we are hereby gracioufly *Strictnefs*
pleafed further to declare to all our *of Difci-*
faid *Admirals, Commanders* in *chief*, and *culcated,*
private *Commanders*, that as our *Royal* *with pro-*
Expectation will from henceforward *mife of*
be, to have a ftrict *Account* given us *yet more*
of their careful applying themfelves *lar marks*
to the Execution and Obfervance of *of the*
thefe and all other our *Orders*, with *Kings*
intention of expreffing our fevereft *upon any*
Difpleafure againft fuch of them (*who-* *fignal in-*
ever *ftances*

ever they be) as fhall be found in any
wife negligent or unfaithful in the
fame. So are we no lefs gracioufly
determined at the *End* of their refpective *Voyages,* to Teftifie by fome
efpecial Inftance of our *Bounty* (beyond
what is hereby already fo *Extraordina-
rily* provided for them) our particular
Regard to whoever of our faid *Commanders* fhall appear to have merited
the fame from us, by any fignal Inftances of their *Induftry, Courage, Conduct*
or *Frugality* evidenced therein on our
behalf. Given at our Court at *Windfor*
this 15th. day of *July* 1686.

By his Majefties Command.

S. PEPYS.

*Return to
the Ships.*
𝖂𝖍𝖎𝖈𝖍 Act having been here obferv'd, out of the *Refpect* no lefs due
to the *Care* at the fame time taken
for the *Re-eftablifhment* of good *Gover-
nance* upon his Majefties Ships *abroad,*
than the *Repair* and *Prefervation* of
thofe in *Port;* the Order of thefe
Notes calls for my Return to the
Works

Works in doing upon the latter, and my obferving thereon, as follows, *Viz*.

That the *fatisfaction* his Majefty was pleas'd to conceive from the fore-mentioned *Progrefs* of thefe *Works*, confirm'd by his own frequent *Vifits*, and *Perfonal Infpections* thereinto at the *Yards*, was fuch, as mov'd him (*fix Months* within the time allow'd for it by the *Propofition*) to think them fo far advanc'd, as not to need his any longer continuing the *Sufpenfion* he had for their fakes laid (as before) upon the *Ordinary Methods* of his Navy. And therefore by his great Seal of the 12*th*. of *Octob*. 1688. (after having declar'd his Gracious *Acceptance* and *Approval* of the Services of thefe his *Commiffioners*, in the full Execution of the *Propofition*, and their having brought all matters intrufted to them, into fuch a *Method*, as that his *Officers* might now perform them, more to his *Service*, than formerly they could) He was pleas'd to determine the *Com-miffion*,

The Kings fatisfaction in the works done thereon.

From his perfonal Vifits to theYards, &c.

Octob. 12.1688. *The Execution of the Com-miffion approved and con-firmed.*

He deter-
mines the
Commif-
fion and
recals the
Old Offi-
cers.

miffion, and recal his faid *Officers* to their ancient *Duties*, according to the known *Inftructions* already in force, and the *Improvements* made therein by thefe *Gentlemen*; inculcating to them his former Directions for the finifhing of their *Accounts*. Among which was in particular that of the *Thirty New Ships*, whereof (but for the *Revolution* immediately following in the *State*) a ftrict *Account* had been foon call'd for, and infifted on by the *King*; as being now (from the through knowledge fince attained concerning them) in a condition of being regularly and effectually controll'd.

Remind
ing them
of their
Old Ac-
counts.

Effects of
this Com-
miffion

And fo expir'd this *Commiffion*; and with what *Effects*, in reference to that diverfity of *Services* for which it was Calculated, and (above all) that one of the general Redemption of the *Fleet* of *England* from Ruin, will be beft underftood, by looking back to the *State* thereof juft before its open-ing in *January* $168\frac{5}{6}$, compar'd with what it was left in at this its *Deter-mination*

In the
ftate it
then left
the Navy
in.

mination in *October* 1688. Which latter follows, *Viz.*

I. The *Fleet* then at *Sea* had (from its ordinary *Summer-Guard*) been rais'd in lefs than two Months (upon intelligence of the furprifing Preparations then on foot in *Holland*) to no lefs than *fixty feven* of the *King's* own *Ships* of *War*, and *Fire-Ships* (befides *Tenders*, *Yachts*, and other fmall Imbarcations) of the Rates following.

Fleet at Sea, Oct. 1688. *raifed upon fhort warning.*

𝕬𝖇𝖘𝖙𝖗𝖆𝖈𝖙 *of the* Fleet *at* Sea *at the clofe of the* Commiffion *of the* Navy, October 1688.

Man'd with above 12000 Men.

		N°.	Men.
	3*d.*	12	4715
Rates—	4	28	6318
	5	2	220
	6	5	370
Fire-Ships		20	680
	Total—	67	12303

II. All

Ships in Harbour how repair'd.

II. **All** but *Three* of the whole remaining *Number* (contain'd in the *Propofition*) entirely repair'd, or actually under Repair; with a furplufage of *fix Months* Time, and a fufficiency of *Mony* and *Materials* refting in *Bank* and *Magazine* for compleating that *Remainder*.

Works how perform'd.

Shewn by the excefs of Charge expended thereon.

III. The *well-performance* of which Works (both for *Extent* and *Subftantialnefs*) had for its firft *Evidence*, the *Sum* expended thereon, to more by two Thirds than the higheft Value the *Surveyor* of the Navy, and his *Fellow-Officers* had Eftimated, and the *Propofition* (grounded on thofe *Eftimates*) Calculated the fame at; divers of them (to above *Thirty*) having been entirely *Rebuilt*, and fome taken up *Hundreds*, others *Thoufands* of Pounds in their *Refitting*, that had but few Months before (without ever going out of *Harbour*) been reprefented by the faid *Officers* to have received from them a *full Repair*.

To which *Proof*, arifing from the
Extra-

Extraordinariness of the *Sum* spent upon them, succeeds that other *Ordinary* one of the *Reports* of the *Master Builders* and their *Assistants*, employ'd in the Direction, and immediate Supervisure thereof. The Names of whom follow. *And by the Reports of the Kings Master Builders and Assistants.*

A List of all his *Majesties* Master *Shipwrights* and their *Assistants* serving him in his several *Yards* between *April* 1686. and *October* 1688.

Wherein Note † *signifies Dead and* * *Preferred.*

Yards.	Mr. Shipwrights.	Assistants.
Chath.	Mr. *Robert Lee*	{ * *Dan. Furzer* *Edw. Dummer* *Phineas Pett*
Portf.	Mr. *Isaac Betts.*	*Wm. Stiggant*
Dept.	{ † Mr. *John Shish* Mr. *Fish. Harding* }	* *Fish. Harding* *Zach. Medbury*
Woolw.	{ † Mr. *Tho. Shish* Mr. *Jos. Lawrence* }	
Sheern.	{ * Mr. *J. Lawrence* Mr. *Dan. Furzer* }	

Persons

Ad-
vanc'd
for their
abilities
under K.
Charles.

Persons, who (besides their having long before the *Date* of this *Commission*, or any occasion fore-seen for it, been from the Credit of their *Abilities* advanc'd to these Charges in the time of *K. Charles*) had not only been all

And em-
ploy'd
Origin-
ally in
surveying
the Fleets
Decays,
and now
in their
Repairs.

of them employ'd by the *Navy-Officers* themselves in taking the very *Surveys* upon which the *Estimates* of the Fleet's Decays were Calculated, and thereby rendred themselves the most concern'd to justifie the same by suitable Performances thereof, both as to Charge and efficacy; but the **Persons** upon whose *Testimonies*, and theirs only, in

Whereof
being the
only pos-
sible
judges,
they alone
by Duty
and Prac-
tice stand
account-
able for
them.

right and virtue of their *Places*, under the *Inspection* of the *Surveyor* of the Navy and *Commissioners* of the Yards (among whom in particular he at *Chatham* was at this time, for the importance of the Works there, one of the first Form of the *Master Builders* of *England*) the Crown always *has*, now *does*, and *for ever must* depend for its security in this *Matter*; as being (in a word) the **Persons**, who by the
Prac-

Practice of the *Navy* ſtand *alone charg'd
with*, by their *Perſonal* ſervices can
alone be *knowing Judges of*, and by the
ſtanding *Obligations* of their *Places* do
therefore *alone* reſt *accountable*, and
(as ſuch) are only to be reſorted to
by the Crown for its ſatisfaction, in
this *Particular*.

IV. Not only the ſix requir'd by
the *Propoſition*, but a compleat *Proportion* of eight Months *Sea-Stores* were
actually provided and left by theſe
Gentlemen in *Magazine* (each within
its Diſtinct and proper *Repoſitory*) for
every Ship ſo repaired ; with the like
in Materials and Mony for the whole
Remainder, as faſt as finiſh'd.

*Every
repaired
Ship fur-
niſh'd
with 8
Months
Sea
Stores.*

And not only ſo ; but in conſider-
ation of the different and uncertain
Meaſures by which *Boatſwains* and
Carpenters of *Ships* had been heretofore ſupply'd (ſometimes too ſparingly
with regard to the Kings Service, other
whiles too largely with reſpect to his
Purſe) they made it their Work (upon
beſt Information) to digeſt and ſee

*The un-
certain
Meaſures
thereof
adjuſted,
aſcer-
tain'd,
and en-
larg'd.*

con-

confirm'd by his *Majesty*, one uniform
Establishment of *Sea-Stores* for an Officer
of each Rate; and that so ample
a one, as to be thought sufficient for
answering (upon occasion) a yet longer
Expence than what it was strictly Calculated for.   So as (to give it in *their*
own Terms to the *King* (*We hope your*
Majesty will from henceforward hear no
more of the many Evils attending the
former Practice. Especially; if the Good
Husbandry *of Your* Commanders *shall*
bear any Proportion to that Mark of
Bounty, *which by your Late* Establishment *you have been pleas'd to grant for*
their Encouragement *thereto.*

And yet to this so inlarged a Proportion of *Stores* set apart for every
particular Ship (and amounting, with
them at Sea, to above two hundred
and fourscore Thousand pounds) they
still added (beyond all *Example*) and
left entirely in *Magazine*, such a further *Reserve* for answering the general
Service of the *Navy*, as amounted in
eight only *Species* thereof, to above

Benefit
thereof to
the King,

Com-
manders
doing
their part.

Besides
which
Sea-stores
to each
Ship,
a general
Maga-
zine is ¹
left,
valued
together
at near
400000 *l.*

¹ *is add.* S. P.   *one*

one hundred thousand pounds more ; *Com-modities* all of greateſt importance and leaſt to be depended-upon from the *Market*, as being (ſave one) all of *Forreign* Growth, *viz.*

Hemp.	*Canvas.*
Pitch.	*Iron.*
Tar.	*Oyle.*
Roſin.	*Wood.*

V. And for the ſafer keeping and more orderly diſpoſing of this laſt-mentioned *Treaſure*, by preventing the Waſtes, Corruption, Imbezlements, and other the manifold miſchiefs attend-ing the want of proper and ſufficient *Store-Room*, occaſion'd by the conſtant *Growth* of the *Naval* Action of *England*, without ſuitable inlargements to its other *Accommodations*; More new *Mag-azines* have (both as to *Dimenſions*, *Contents*, and *Charge*) been erected within the two years and a half of this *Commiſſion*, than had ever been before, by all the *Kings* of *England* put together.

Store-Room, much wanting in the Navy. Supply'd by new Erections beyond all it ever had before.

VI. Nor

VI. Nor are the foremention'd *Advances* in these works less owing to the *industry* successfully exercised in the improvement of our *Docks*, than in that of the *Magazines*, by bettering the *Old*, and finishing the *New*; to the raising them to the *State* they are now left in, Superiour to all that the *Navy* of *England* ever before knew. And yet not more then its present Occasions call'd for, as not having permitted any one of them to lye unimploy'd two *Tides* together (while in condition for it) within the whole time.

A suitable improvement of the Docks, and not less wanting.

VII. *Four* and *Twenty* of *Seven* and *Twenty* of his Majesty's *Ships* and *Vessels*, come in from *Sea* during this *Commission*, and therefore (as being then abroad) not provided for in the *Proposition*, have been also fully *repair'd* or left actually under *Repair*, furnish'd with like proportion of *Sea-Stores* (as before) without a Penny supply'd out of the Exchequer towards it.

Ships come home, repair'd and stored, though not of the Proposition.

And

And in the doing this, that moſt *And this within the Rate in the Propoſition of 22 s. for Wear and Tear.* important (and till now unheard of) *Article* at the Cloſe of the *Propoſition,* relating to the future maintenance of his *Majeſties Fleets* at *Sea* in their whole *Wear* and *Tear,* at *no higher* charge than that of 22 *s. per* Man a Month, has been alſo made good; and, in that *ſingle* performance, a Foundation *Saving for ever the whole firſt Coſt of New-building, and 26 per Cent in all ſucceeding Charges upon the Bodies of the Ships.* laid of ſaving to the Crown for ever, not only the whole *firſt Coſt* of what- ever Ships it shall have occaſion of building in lieu of others become *irre- pairable*; but twenty ſix *per Cent* in the Charge of all ſucceeding Repairs and Expence in their Stores and Furniture.

VIII. Every other Head of the *Pro- poſition* ſtrictly comply'd with, the *Nothing undone of the Propo- ſition, but two of the ſmall Frigats reſpited by Order.* Building of two ſmall *Frigats* only ex- cepted, which by expreſs Command of the *King* were reſpited (and the Value of them therefore left uncall'd-for out of the *Treaſury*) till the weightier Works of his great *Ships* would allow *Room* and *Leaſure* for their being built in his own Yards.

IX. Not

IX. Not a *Penny* left unpaid to any *Officer, Seaman, Workman, Artificer* or *Merchant,* for any *Service* done in, or *Commodity* deliver'd to the ufe of the *Navy,* either at Sea or on Shore, within the whole time of this *Commiffion,* where the *Party* claiming the fame was in the way to receive it, and had (if an *Accountant*) done his part, as fuch, towards the entitling himfelf to Payment.

Even in which Cafe too, a fufficiency of *Cafh* was left in *Bank* upon the Fond of this *Commiffion,* for clearing that *Debt,* as faft as by the Coming in of *Ships,* and adjuftment of *Accounts,* the fame could be brought into a *Capacity* and *Right* of being paid.

X. Laftly, The whole of this *Propofition* was thus made good, and therewith the *Navy* of *England* redeem'd from perifhing, at a *Charge* not only not exceeding the 400000 *l.* per *Ann.* allotted for it by the *King,* and confequently not more than what the *Navy* appear'd (as before) to have

been

been fupply'd with all the time of its being fo abandon'd to *Ruine*, but even for lefs than 310000 l. *per Annum* ; as the fame ftands verify'd by the *Verify'd* *Accounts* thereof in the *Regiftry* of the *by the* *Navy*, and thofe Accounts (both as *Accounts thereof.* to Truth and Perfpicuity (fo digefted, juftify'd, and (after the Clofe of each year) prefented to the *King* and his *Treasurers*, anfwering in every refpect the Scope of the *Propofition*, by dif- tinct Reckonings exhibited therein of every *Species* and parcel of *Goods* bought and fpent, *Artificer* and *Work- man* employ'd, *Penny* laid out, and *Service* perform'd (with the Difference or Agreement in the Charge of every fuch *Service* with its proper *Eftimate*) as does not appear to have ever before been feen in the *Navy* of *England*, but (through the fingle *Induftry* and peculiar *Conduct* of Mr. *Hewer*) is now remaining there, to fhew *Pofterity*, that there is nothing in the *Nature*, *Bulk*, or *Diverfity* of Matters incident to the bufinefs of a *Navy* (even under the circumftances of *this*) to juftifie the fo-long-admitted Pretence of an *Irreducibleneſs* of its *Accounts*, to a degree of *Order* and *Self-Evidence* equal to the moft ftrict of any private Merchant.

General State of the Account upon this Propofition, &c.

The general *State* of which *Accounts* in the Cafe of the prefent *Propofition*, and the *Works* attending it (as the fame arifes from the *fubordinate Accounts* relative thereto) follows.

Which

A General STATE *of* ACCOUNT, *Relating to the* 4000
of the NAVY, *for answering Mr.* Pepys's PROPOSITION; *As*
Extraordinary *in the* NAVY, *under the Late* Commiſſion be
two Years, Six Months and two Weeks; according to Parti

				£.	s.	d

<table>
<tr><td colspan="5">The Exchequer to the Navy is</td><td>Dr.</td></tr>
</table>

The Exchequer to the Navy is   Dr.

£.   s.   d

The *Propofition* of 400000 l. *per Ann.*, affign'd for the particular } *Works* and *Services* efpecially nam'd therein ———   1015384 : 12 : 0

To fo much upon

Extraordinary *Works* and *Services* perform'd in purfuance of fpecial *Articles* in the faid *Propofition*, not chargeable upon the 400000. l. *viz.*

The *Excefs* of Charge in the *Repairs* of Ships and Veſſels beyond the *Eſtimates* thereof made by the *Officers* of the *Navy*, according to the 2*d.* Article of the faid *Propofition.* —— £. 82870.

The like *Excefs* (according to the 2*d.* and 3*d.* Articles of the fame) in the Charge of *Rigging*, and Boatfwains and Carpenters *Sea-ftores* beyond their *Eſtimate.* —— 41016.

The Value of *Ware*, and *Tear* of 24 Ships and Veſſels repair'd, equipp'd, and furniſh'd with *Sea-ftores*, computed but at 22*s.* per Man a Month, according to the *fupplemental Article* in the *Propofition* relating to *Ships* at *Sea* upon the 25*th.* of *March* 1686. that fhould come in during this *Commiſſion.* —— 76600.

200486 : 00 : 00

Extraordinary Works and *Services* done by *Order*, neither provided for, nor mention'd in the *Propofition*, fuch as (among others) the *Erecting* the feveral *Store-houfes*, and other *New ftructures* in the *Yards*; the Magazines of *Stores*, provided for the *General fervice* of the Navy, over and above the 8 Months *Sea-ftores* fet apart for each *Ship*; and the *Excefs* of Charge in *Victuals* and otherwife upon the *Ships* fet out for the Lord *Dartmouth's* Fleet in *Auguft* and *September* 1688, above the 4000 *Men* provided for in the *Propofition*, &c.   178905 : 01 : 07

From *Total* ———— 1394775 : 13 : 07

Take the Credit-fide— 1087205 : 04 : 03

Exchequer remains *Debtor* to the *Navy* upon this *Account*, } over and above the 121292 *l. per Contrà.* ——— 307570 : 09 : 04

Per Contrà		*Cr.*

£. s. d.

Payd to the Treasurer of the Navy in part of the 1015384. 12. 00. } per Contrà ———   849670 : 0 : 0.

Credit to be given this *Account,* according to the *2d. 3d.* and *5th.* Articles of the *Propofition* for

    So much *lefs* expended in the *Repair* of feveral Ships, than they were *Eftimated* at ———   *£.* 17385.

    The *Value* of the *Eftimates* wholly unexpended upon Ships judged *irrepairable* ———   6553.

    The *Value* of the *Eftimates* of three Ships remaining ftill to be *repaired,* viz. ———   8138.

         £.
         Prince ——— 4329.
         Victory ——— 2841.
         Royal-Oake ——— 968.

    The *Value* of the *Hulls* of two of the fmall *Frigats* forborn to be built by the fpecial Command of His *Majefty.* ———   6000.

} 38076 : 0 : 0.

    More *paid* to the *Treafurer* of the *Navy* in part of the 178905 : 1 : 7. *per Contrà.* ———   66167 : 4 : 3

    More *chargeable* on the faid *Treafurer* for the Proceed of feveral *Ships* and *Veffels* fold as decay'd and unferviceable; with other *extraordinary fums* in further part of the 178905 : 1 : 7 *per Contrà.* ———   12000 : 0 : 0

} 78167 : 4 : 3.

    So much left *unpay'd* by the *Commiffion* at the *Determination* thereof (with its Value left in the *Exchequer* upon the *Fond* of the *Propofition* for defraying the fame,) ——— *Viz.*

                      l.

Upon   *Wages* to the   *Ships* at Sea ——— 104132.
                Yards ——— 8500.
     Bills for *Stores, Workmanfhip, &c.* unadjufted — 8660.

   121292 : 0 : 0.

Total ——— 1087205 : 4 : 3

𝖂𝖍𝖎𝖈𝖍 *State* of *Accounts* being (as it ought) admitted, in right to its *Vouchers* now resting (as from the very *Close* of this *Commission* they have done) in the *hands* of the so often-mentioned *Officers* of the *Navy*, who (after what has been here said) cannot but be esteem'd in *Honour* the most concern'd, as well as by *Duty* the most oblig'd, to see the same fully *controll'd*; these (among other *Particulars* no less considerable) offer themselves to Observation, *viz.*

The Officers of the Navy possessed of the Vouchers of this Account, and most concerned to see it controlled.

Observables from this Account.

1. That the 307000 *l.* the *Ballance* of this *Account*, is the *Product* of these Gentlemens *Management*; as being so much saved of what might unexceptionably have been expended by them, out of the 400000 *l. Fond* assigned to the use of this *Proposition.*

307000l. saved upon the Proposition.

2. That among the several other immediate and important *Fruits* of this *Saveing*, this is one; namely, the obtaining such an Enlargement of *Magazines*, and the amassing therein such a *Treasure* of *Stores*, as *England* was never before *Mistress* of, nor

Fruits of this Saving.

could

could now have had its *Navy* longer
supported without.

*Charge
of this
Manage-
ment com-
pared
with the
last.*

3. *Lastly,* That this and all the
above-mentioned *Advantages* have
been effected at no other *Cost,* than
the bare *Wages* of the few His
Majesty was pleas'd to call to this
his Service, arising together to little
more than 6000 *l.* While (had the
Work been transacted by *Contract*) the
whole of that 307000 *l. Ballance* must
incontestably have been the *Reward*
of the *Undertakers*; and the *Bargain*
nevertheless not reckon'd any un-
thrifty one to the *Publick,* when it
should be consider'd, that the Execution of this *Proposition* (with the many
Benefits attending it) within less than
three years, would (even with that
Sum included) have barely amounted
to **One** *Million* ; while *five* entire years
were lost, and the *Navy* all that time
left under little less than a total
Defertion, at the Expence (as before)
of full **Two.** And of that also
(without offence be it observ'd) near
Five and *thirty thousand Pounds* taken
up

up in *Wages* only, to a *Commiſſion* of
the *Admiralty*, during that very Management; While this appears exempt
of the *Charge* of any ſuch *Commiſſion*,
or ought elſe extraordinary to the
value of a *Shilling*, beyond the Simple
Wages of a worn unaſſiſted SECRETARY.

And yet with ſuch *Effect* too; that *And the*
from the *Condition* the *Navy* was (by *different*
its own Officers) reported in, at His *Effects*
Majeſty's Reſuming it in 1684, when *thereof.*
the *Groſs* of its *Ships* were wholly out
of *Repair*, and the beſt of them ready
to *ſink* in *Harbour*, with little appearance of its having by this time had
any one of them in a *State* of *Service*;
it has the preſent *Reputation* (1690) of
having *actually* at *Sea* of its own *Ships*
of *War* and *Fire-ſhips* (excluſive of
Merchant-men and *Forreigners*) a *Force*
equal at leaſt, or rather ſuperior, to
the moſt *powerful* it ever at any one
time had, in the moſt *active* year of
a *Hollands-War*. And (which is more)
the *Reſidue* (as to their *Hulls* and
Stores) in a ready *State* of following
them, if (as I am not to doubt) the
                                        ſame

fame *wholefom Methods* have been fince exercis'd towards them, with thofe they were brought-by into the *Condition* this *Commiffion* left them in, upon the 12th of *October*, 1688.

Which leading me back to the fore-mentioned *State* of this *Affair* in *October*; little refts for the carrying it on to that *fignal Day*, that puts a natural *Bound* to the *fubject* of thefe *Notes*, I mean the *Day* of my late *Royal* (but moft unhappy) *Mafter's* Retiring in *December*; As having received little other *Alteration* within that time, than what arofe from a fmall *Addition* to the *Fleet* under the Lord *Dartmouth*, and the coming home of fome few others from *Forreign Service*; rendering the *whole* then abroad, as follows,

The State of the Fleet in October 1688. *carried on to the Day of the King's withdrawing himfelf in* December.

Abftract *of the* Ships *of* War *and* Fire-Ships *in* Sea-Pay *upon the* 18th *of* December, 1688.

Manned with above 14600 Men.

Rate

	Ships			Men.	
	At Sea.	Going out.	Total		*Ships at Sea in December 1688.*
Rate ⎰3d	10	5	15	6080	
⎱4	29	2	31	7015	
5	2	0	2	220	
6	4	0	4	295	
Fire-Ships	22	4	26	965	
Bomber	1	0	1	75	
Total	68	11	79	14650	

𝕿𝖍𝖊 *Import* of which *Fleet*, at a *Crisis* so eminent, as this is likely to appear in the future *Annals* of *England* (when it shall be remembred what passed, besides it, upon the *British-Seas* between the two last-cited Periods of *October* and *December*) seeming to require some more distinct *Report* of it, than what is to be gathered from the foregoing *Abstracts*; I subjoyn a *List*, specifying the *Rate*, *Name*, *Officers*, *Complement* of *Men* and *Station* of every Ship and Vessel of His *Majesty*'s then in *Sea-Service*, viz.

The same Reported more particularly, for the sake of what occurr'd in our Seas within that Interval.

A

A *General* **List** of all His Majesty's
Pay, upon the 18th of *December,* 1688.
Lieutenants, Complements of *Men,* and

Rates	Ships	Commanders
3d	*Resolution*————	L. *Dartmouth* Ad. C. *Davis*————
3	*Elizabeth*————	S. *J. Berry* V. Ad. C. *Nevill*——
3	*Cambridge*————	C. *Tyrwhit*——
3	*Defiance*————	C. *Ashby*——
3	*Dreadnought*——	C. *Akarman*——
3	*Henrietta*————	C. *Trevanion*——
3	*Mary*————	C. *Layton*——
3	*Pendennis*————	Sir *Will. Booth*
3	*Plymouth*————	C. *Carter*——
3	*York*————	C. *Delavall*——
4th	*Advice*————	C. *Williams*——
4	*Albans* Saint——	C. *Constable*——
4	*Anthelope*————	C. *Ridley*——

Ships and *Vessels* in *Sea-Service* and with their respective *Rates, Commanders, Stations.*

Lieutenants	Men	Station
{ *Millison* ———) { *Preene* ———)	450	
(*Gother* ———) { *Crawley* ——— }	475	
(*Wrigh* ———) { *Bois* ———)	420	
(*Bing* ———) { *Littleton* ———)	390	
(*Bounty* ———) { *Tyrwhit* ——— }	355	
(*Gardner* ———) { *Dilks* ——— }	355	
(*Townesend* ——) { *Hays* ——— }	355	} Channel
(*Jennings* ———) { *Kerr* ———)	460	
(*Foulks* ———) { *Edwards* ———)	340	
(*Moody* ———) { *Manley* ——— }	340	
Haughton ———	230	
(*Killigrew* ——) { *Bundee* ———)	280	
Pugh ———	230	

Rates	Ships	Commanders
4th	Assurance———	C. Mack Donell.
4	Bonadventure———	C. Hopson———
4	Bristoll———	C. Leighton———
4	Centurion———	C. Elliot———
4	ConstantWarwick	C. Cornwall———
4	Crown———	C. Robinson———
4	David Saint———	C. Botham———
4	Deptford———	C. Rook———
4	Diamond———	C. Walters———
4	Dover———	C. Shovel———
4	Foresight———	C. Standley———
4	Greenwich———	C. Wrenn———
4	Jersey———	C. Beverly———
4	Mordaunt———	C. Tyrrell———
4	New Castle———	C. Churchill———
4	Nonsuch———	C. Montgomery
4	Phœnix———	C. Gifford———
4	Portland———	C. G. Aylemore
4	Portsmouth———	C. St. Loe———
4	Ruby———	C. Froud———
4	Swallow———	C. M. Aylemore
4	Tiger———	C. Tennant———

Lieutenants	Men	Station
Fitz Patrick	180	
Granvil	230	
{ Penn / Townsend }	230	
	230	
Hales	180	
Wickham	230	
{ Jennings / Walker }	280	
{ Guy / Bowyer }	280	
Greenway	230	
Dawes	230	
{ Hubbard / Man }	230	Channel
{ Vaughan / Audeley }	280	
Hammond	230	
Carveth	230	
Harman	280	
Talbot	180	
Harrison	180	
Trevanion	240	
Beaumont	220	
Gillam	230	
Whittaker	230	
L. Will. Murray	230	

Rates	Ships	Commanders
4th	*Woolwich*———	C. *Haſtings*———
6	*Lark*———	C. *Grimſditch*—
6	*Saudados*———	C. *Graydon*———
Bomb.	*Fire Drake*———	C. *Leake*———
Ketch	*Quaker*———	C. *Allin*———
	Cleveland———	C. *Hoskins*———
	Fubbs———	C. *R. Sanderſon*
Yts.	*Iſabella*———	C. *W. Sanderſon*
	Katherine———	C. *Clements*———
	Kitchin———	C. *Crow*———
	Mary———	C. *Fazeby*———
	Cygnet———	C. *Shelley*———
	Dartmouth———	C. *Legg*
	Elizab and *Sarah*	C. *Dover*———
	Guardland———	C. *Jenifer*———
	Richard & *John*—	C. *Will Wright*
	Supply———	C. *Croſſe*———
	Guernſey———	C. *Arthur*———
F.Sh.	*Pearl*———	C. *Coale*———
	Richmond———	C. *Fairborne*———
	Swan———	C. *Johnſon*———
	Sophia———	C. *Mings*———
	Speedwell———	C. *Powſon*———
	Roſe Salley Prize	
	Saint *Paul*———	C. *Boteler*———
	Charles & *Henry*	C. *Stone*———

Lieutenants	Men	Station
{*Talmach*———} {*Baker*———}	280	Channel
	85	
	75	
	75	
	40	
	30	
	40	
	30	
	30	
	30	
	30	
	30	
	55	
	25	
	50	
	20	
	20	
	50	
	50	
	50	
	50	
	27	
	30	
	37	
	50	
	25	

Rate	Ships	Commanders
F.Sh. {	Roebuck	C. *Pooley*
	Unity	C. *Wyvel*
	Charles	C. *Potter*
	Half-moon	C. *Munden*
	Young Spragg	C. *Wiseman*
Yacht	Merlin	C. *Wilde*
F.Sh. {	Eagle	C. *Willford*
	Sampson	C. *Harris*
Yacht	Navy	C. *Cotton*
Ketch	Kingfisher	C. *Swaine*
Yacht	Monmouth	C. *Will.Wright*
4th	Dragon	C. *Killigrew*
4	Sedgemore	C. *Lloyd*
5	Saphire	C. *Tosier*
Hulk	Leopard	
4	Assistance	C. *Law.Wright*
6	Drake	C. *Spragg*
5	Rose	C. *George*
Ketch	Deptford	C. *Berry*
6	Dunbarton	C. *Roe*

Lieutenants	Men	Station
	16	}
	25	Channel
	30	
	35	
	20	} Portsm. }
	30	Guard
	45	} Sheern.
	50	
	20	Guernsey
	15	Jersey
	20	Ireland
{Bokenham——}{Sherborne——}	185	}
{Buckely——}{Hawkins——}	240	} Salley
Brisbane——	115	
	33	
Chapman——	200	} Jamaica
	65	
Condon——	105	New-England
	40	} Virginia
	70	

Ships

		Ships just come-in
Rate	Ships	Commanders
3d	*Montague*————	L.*Berkley*,R.Ad.
3	*Rupert*————	Sir *Will Jennens*

		Ships go-
Rate	Ships	Commanders
3d	*Edgar*————	L.*Berkley*,R.Ad.
3	*Dunkirk*————	
3	*Warspight*————	Sir*Will Jennens*
3	*Hampton-Court*—	C. *Priestman*—
3	*Kent*————	Sir *F. Wheeler*—
4	*Tiger* Prize————	C. *Smith*
4	*Sweepstakes* ———	
F. Sh. ⎨	*Mermaid*————	C. *Ley*—
	Thomas & *Eliz.* ———	
	Owners Love———	
	Cadiz Merchant—	

to be exchanged.

Lieutenants	Men	Station
Conway Every Staggins Day	355 400	Channel.

ing out.

Lieutenants	Men	Station
Every	460	
	340	
	420	
Buck	460	
Usher	460	Channel.
Foules	230	
	80	
	50	
	40	
	40	
	45	

Abstract of the preceding List			
Rates and Qualities	Ships		Men
	At Sea	Going out	Total	
Rates ⎰ 3d—	10	5	15	6080
⎱ 4—	29	2	31	7015
5—	2	0	2	220
6—	4	0	4	295
Firefhips——	22	4	26	965
Bomber——	1	0	1	75
Hulk——	1	0	1	33
Ketches——	3	0	3	95
Yachts——	9	0	9	260
Total——	81	11	92	15038

And

And to the end nothing may be wanting to render thefe *Notes* completely expreffive of the *State*, not of that *Fleet* only, but of the whole *Navy* of *England* at this fo extraordinary *Conjuncture*, I add one *Table* more, fhewing (through all the principal[1] *Circumftances* of it) the particular *Condition*, wherein every *Ship* and *Veffel* thereof then ftood, with the united *Force* of the *Whole*, as follows, *viz*.

A General Lift and State of the whole Navy of England, December 18, 1688.

principal] principle *ed.*

H 2   A

A
LIST and STATE
OF THE
ROYAL NAVY

A

A **List** and

Of the whole ROYAL NAVY of *Harbour*) upon the 18. day of *dition* of each *Ship* and *Vessel pairs* and the Value of their day; containing also an *Account* presented to his *Majesty* by the of every *Ship* comprehended par'd with the *Real Charge* of the late *Commissioners* of the *Navy*, *Commission March* 25th. 1686. and

Wherein to

That the *Ships* { Mark'd { *A.* were at *Sea* *B.* were in *Har-* *C.* have been in the **Black** Letter are

State

England (whether at *Sea* or in
December 1688. ſhewing the *Con-*
therein, with reſpect to their *Re-*
Rigging and *Sea Stores,* upon that
of the laſt and higheſt *Eſtimates*
Officers of his *Navy* of the *Defects*
within *Mr. Pepys's Propoſition*; com-
Works perform'd thereon by the
between the *Commencement* of their
its *Determination October* 12. 1688.

be noted,

upon——————————— ⎫ the ſaid 25
bour wanting repair, on—— ⎬ of *March*
added to the *R. Navy,* ſince ⎭ 1686.
the 30 *New Ships.*

Ships

Ships and Vessels.	Place and Condition		
	At Sea or going forth.	In Har-	
		re-pair'd.	*Under Repair.*
1st. Rate.			
St. Andrew	B	*	
Brittannia	B		*
Charles Royal	B	*	
George St.	B		*
James Royal	B	*	
London	B	*	
Michael St.	B		*
Prince Royal	B		
Soveraign	B	*	
2d. Rate.			
Albemarle	B	*	
Coronation	B	*	
Duke	B	*	
Dutchess	B	*	
Katherine	B		*
Neptune	B	*	
Ossory	B	*	

Dec. 18. 1688.				
bour.		*Estimates of their Defects.*	*Real charge of their Repairs.*	*Value of their Rigging and Sea Stores.*
To be re-pair'd.	*Newly come in from Sea.*			
		£.	£.	£.
		1616	1650	4296
		2315	2138	5181
		1577	1646	4735
		1918	—	4296
		1400	1882	4735
		796	1574	4296
		1286	5092	3668
*		—		4735
		2134	1349	5181
		13042	15331	41123
		3213	3773	4296
		1200	1327	4296
		719	2862	4296
		1193	2826	4296
		1499	2081	3668
		949	1622	4296
		837	745	4296

Ships and Vessels.	Place and *Condition*		
	At Sea or going forth.	In Har-	
		re-pair'd.	*Under Repair.*
Sandwich	B	*	
Vanguard	B	*	
Victory	B		
Windsor Castle	B	*	
3d. Rate.			
Anne	B	*	
Berwick	B	*	
Bredah	B	*	
Burford	B	*	
Cambridge	B *		
Captain	B	*	
Defiance	B *		
Dreadnought	B *		
Dunkirk	B *		
Eagle	B	*	
Edgar	B *		
Elizabeth	B *		

Dec. 18. 1688. bour.		Estimates of their Defects.	Real charge of their Repairs.	Value of their Rigging and Sea Stores.
To be re-pair'd.	Newly come in from Sea.	£.	£.	£.
———	———	1622	3015	4296
	———	897	1027	4296
*	———			3668
———	———	650	3438	4296
		12779	22716	46000
———	———	862	2203	2976
———	———	1055	370	2976
———	———	1186	1742	2976
———	———	975	2165	2976
———	———	944	4999	2580
———	———	1215	3046	2976
———	———	512	1747	2365
———	———	1140	1780	2195
———	———	409	592	1903
———	———	705	586	2976
———	———	1911	7141	2976
———	———	503	1444	2976

Ships and Vessels.		Place and *Condition*		
			In Har-	
		At Sea or going forth.	*re-pair'd.*	*Under Repair.*
Essex	B		*	
Exeter	B		**	
Expedition	B		**	
Grafton	B		**	
Hampt. Court	B	*		
Harwich	B		*	
Henrietta	B	*		
Hope	B		*	
Kent	B	*		
Lenox	B		**	
Lion	B		**	
Mary	B	*		
Monck	B			*
Monmouth	B		*	
Montague	B		**	
Northumberl.	B		**	
Royal Oak	B			
Pendennis	B	*		
Plymouth	B	**		
Resolution	B	**		

Dec. 18. 1688.				
bour.		Estimates of their Defects.	Real charge of their Repairs.	Value of their Rigging and Sea Stores.
To be re-pair'd.	Newly come in from Sea.			
		£.	£.	£.
		1427	1454	2976
		1391	553	2976
		725	401	2976
		735	1496	2976
		830	4771	2976
		634	885	2580
		594	945	2195
		1257	1922	2976
		1382	1670	2976
		354	797	2976
		602	955	2195
		3152	7236	2195
		1565	2212	2195
		997	5643	2365
		503	3814	2365
		1186	1114	2976
*		—	—	2976
		736	1521	2976
		670	1111	2195
		510	1292	2365

Ships and Vessels.	Place and Condition		
	At Sea or going forth.	In Har-	
		re-pair'd.	Under repair.
𝕽eſtauration ——— B		*	
Rupert ——— B		*	
𝕾terling-𝕮aſt. ——— B		*	
𝕾uffolk ——— B		*	
Swiftſure ——— B		*	
Warſpight ——— B	*		
York ——— B	*		
4th. Rate.			
Advice ——— B	*		
Albans St. ——— C	*		
Anthelope ——— B	*		
Aſſiſtance ——— B	*		
Aſſurance ——— B	*		
Bonadventure ——— A	*		
Briſtol ——— A	*		
Charles Gally ——— B			
Centurion ——— B	*		

Dec. 18. 1688. bour.		Estimates of their Defects.	Real charge of their Repairs.	Value of their Rigging and Sea Stores.
To be re-pair'd.	Newly come in from Sea.			
		£.	£.	£.
		2969	734	2976
		129	420	2365
		1349	2033	2976
		357	1857	2976
		610	941	2580
		1959	4130	2365
		1460	4147	2165
		39502	81869	104670
		2902	1558	1582
		2212	3597	1582
		1749	2142	1582
		1812	3640	1582
		989	1316	1348
			——	1582
		——	——	1582
	*	186	183	1348
		1222	3498	1582

Ships and Vessels.		Place and Condition		
		At Sea or going forth.	In Har-	
			re-pair'd.	Under Repair.
Constant Warwick	B	*		
Crown	A	*		
David St.	B	*		
Deptford	C	*		
Diamond	B	*		
Dover	B	*		
Dragon	B	*		
Faulcon	A			
Foresight	B	*		
Greenwich	B	*		
Hampshire	B		*	
Happy Return	A			*
James Gally	A		*	
Jersey	B	*		
King-fisher	A			*
Mary Rose	A			
Mary Gally	C		*	
Mordaunt	B	*		
New Castle	B	*		
Nonsuch	B	*		

Dec. 18. 1688.		Estimates of their Defects.	Real charge of their Repairs.	Value of their Rigging and Sea Stores.
bour.				
To be re-pair'd.	Newly come in from Sea.			
		£.	£.	£.
		1189	451	1348
				1582
		210	687	1903
		2377	4596	1728
		576	821	1582
		1849	3043	1582
		748	268	1472
	*			1348
		390	380	1582
		280	374	1903
		2500	3349	1472
				1728
				1348
		2254	1416	1582
				1903
	*			1582
				1348
		642	1025	1582
		1329	2223	1728
		1721	2024	1348

Ships and Vessels.		Place and _Condition_		
		At Sea or going forth.	In Har	
			re-pair'd.	_Under Repair._
Oxford	A			*
Phœnix	A	*		
Portland	B	*		
Portſmouth	B	*		
Reſerve	B			
Ruby	A	*		
Sedgemore	C	*		
Swallow	B	*		
Sweepſtakes	B	*		
Tiger	B	*		
Tiger Prize	B	*		
Woolwich	B	*		
5th. Rate.				
Roſe	A	*		
Saphire	A	*		

Dec. 18. 1688. bour.		Estimates of their Defects.	Real charge of their Repairs.	Value of their Rigging and Sea Stores.
To be re-pair'd.	Newly come in from Sea.			
		£.	£.	£.
		—	—	1903
		—	—	1348
		1922	4689	1728
		2500	2649	1472
	*	427	259	1582
		—	—	1582
		2337	3650	1728
		1314	1571	1582
		1368	1612	1348
		326	365	1728
		1348	1102	1582
		525	1513	2195
		39204	54001	65199
		—	—	902
		—	—	1031
				1933

Ships and Veſſels.		Place and Condition		
		At Sea or going forth.	In Har	
			re-pair'd.	Under Repair.
6th. Rate.				
Drake———	A	✳		
Dunbarton———	B	✳		
Fanfan———	B		✳	
Greyhound———	A		✳	
Larke———	A	✳		
Saudados ———	A	✳		
Bombers				
Fire-Drake———	C	✳		
Portſmouth———	A		✳	
Salamander———	C		✳	
Fire Ships				
Cadiz-Merchant—	C	✳		
Cygnet———	C	✳		
Charles———	C	✳		

Dec. 18. 1688. bour.		*Estimates of their Defects.*	*Real charge of their Repairs.*	*Value of their Rigging and Sea Stores.*
To be re-pair'd.	*Newly come in from Sea.*			
		£.	£.	£.
				536
		156	288	634
		30	36	391
				634
				634
				634
		186	324	3463
				634
				391
				536
				1561
				250
				250

Ships and Vessels.		Place and Condition		
		At Sea or going forth.	In Har	
			re-pair'd.	Under Repair.
Charles and Henry	C	✳		
Dartmouth———	A	✳		
Eagle———	A	✳		
Eliz. and Sarah.-	C	✳		
Guardland———	B	✳		
Guernsey———	B	✳		
Half-Moon———	C	✳		
Mermaid———	A	✳		
Owners Love———	C	✳		
Pearle———	A	✳		
Paul St.———	B	✳		
Rich. and John —	C	✳		
Richmond———	B	✳		
Roebuck———	C	✳		
Rose———	B	✳		
Sampson———	B	✳		
Sophia———	B	✳		
Speedwell———	C	✳		
Supply———	C	✳		
Swann———	B	✳		

Dec. 18. 1688.				
bour.		Estimates of their Defects.	Real charge of their Repairs.	Value of their Rigging and Sea Stores.
To be re-pair'd.	Newly come in from Sea.			
		£.	£.	£.
				273
				1031
				902
				300
		295	147	1031
		1150	1685	1031
				634
				1031
				1031
		630	1014	1031
		590	1403	902
				250
		155	575	902
		520	411	902
		110	182	536
				280
		795	633	1031

Ships and Vessels.		Place and Condition		
		At Sea or going forth.	In Har	
			re-pair'd.	Under Repair.
Thomas and *Eliz.*	C	*	—	
Unity———	C	*	—	
Young Spragg——	B	*	—	
Hoys.				
Delight———	B	—	*	
Lighter———	B	—	*	
Marygold———	B	—	*	
Nonfuch———	C	—	*	
Transporter——	B	—	*	
Unity Horfeboat-	B	—	*	
Hulkes.				
Arms of *Horne*—	B	—	*	
Arms of *Rotterd.*-	B	—	*	
French Ruby——	B	—	*	
George Saint———	B	—	*	

Dec. 18. 1688. bour.		Eſtimates of their Defects.	Real charge of their Repair.	Value of their Rigging and Sea Stores.
To be re-pair'd.	Newly come in from Sea.	£.	£.	£.
				277
		80	126	390
		4325	6176	14265
		129	83	—
		2065	680	—
		1427	193	—

Ships and Vessels.		At Sea, or going forth.	In Har	
			Place and Condition	
			re-pair'd.	Under Repair.
Leopard———	B	*		
Maria Prize———	C	} *Gibr.*		
Puntoone———	B			
State-Houſe———	B		*	
Ketches.				
Deptford———	A	*		
Kingfiſher ———	A	*		
Quaker———	A	*		
Smacks.				
Eſcape Royal———	B		*	
Little London——	B		*	
Sheerneſs———	B		*	
Shiſh———	B		*	
Tow-Engine———	B		*	

Dec. 18. 1688.				
bour.		Eſtimates of their Defects.	Real charge of their Repairs.	Value of their Rigging and Sea Stores.
To be re-pair'd.	Newly come in from Sea.			
		£.	£.	£.
— —	— —	3858	1156	1562
— —	— —			
— —	— —	300	126	— —
		7779	2238	1562
— —	— —	— —	— —	391
— —	— —	— —	— —	391
— —	— —	— —	— —	391
				1173
— —	— —	— —	— —	— —
— —	— —	— —	— —	— —
— —	— —	— —	— —	— —
— —	— —	— —	— —	— —
— —	— —			

Ships and Vessels.		Place and Condition		
		At Sea or going forth.	In Har	
			re-pair'd.	Under Repair
Yachts.				
Charlotte	A		*	
Cleveland	B	*		
Fubbs	A	*		
Henrietta	A		*	
Jemmy	B		*	
Isabella	A	*		
Isle of Wight	B		*	
Katherine	A	*		
Kitchin	A	*		
Mary	A	*		
Merlin	B	*		
Monmouth	A	*		
Navy	A	*		
Quinborow	B		*	

Dec. 18. 1688. bour.		Estimates of their Defects.	Real charge of their Repair.	Value of their Rigging and Sea Stores.
To be re-pair'd.	Newly come in from Sea.	£.	£.	£.
		—	—	550
		—	—	550
		—	—	550
		—	—	550
		—	—	160
		—	—	360
		—	—	100
		—	—	550
		—	—	500
		—	—	550
		—	—	550
		—	—	550
		—	—	400
		—	—	50
				5970

An Abftract of the foregoing *Lift*
England, upon the 18. of *December*

Ships and Veffels.	Place and *Condition*		
	At Sea or going forth.	In Har	
		re-pair'd.	Under Repair.
Rates— { 1.—		5	3
2.—		9	1
3.—	15	22	1
4.—	31	3	3
5.—	2		
6.—	4	2	
Bombers—	1	2	
Firefhips—	26		
Hoys—		6	
Hulks—	1	7	
Ketches—	3		
Smacks—		5	
Yachts—	9	5	
	92	66	8

and *State* of the *Royal Navy* of 1688. with the *Force* of the whole.

| Dec. 18. 1688. bour. | | Force. | | |
To be re-pair'd.	Newly come in from Sea.	Total.	Men.	Guns.
1		9	6705	878
1		11	7010	974
1		39	16545	2640
	4	41	9480	1908
		2	260	60
		6	420	90
		3	120	34
		26	905	218
		6	22	
		8	50	
		3	115	24
		5	18	
		14	353	104
3	4	173	42003	6930

Conclusion.

And having thus summarily brought this *Deduction* of the last *Ten* years *Home-Transactions* of our *Navy* to the day I first set for its *Period,* as it also (most wellcomely) proves to my own (now 30 *Years*) Relation to't; wherein (as an *Englishman,* and in a *Service* purely *English*) I have ever with all simplicity of mind contended, to render this humble *Province* of mine useful to my *Country :* I close this **Paper.**

Which amounting to little more than the *Contents* of one *Chapter* of a greater Number, wherewith the *World* may some time or other be more largely entertain'd upon the general Subject of the *Navalia* of *England;* I have, (for preventing either others or my own being misled, to the *believing* or *reporting* ought herein needing *Animadversion*) chosen to expose what is here said, Now, while

while fo many are furviving, whofe
Memories (joyn'd with the eafie Re-
courfe to be ftill had to the *Original
Regifters* thereof in the *Offices* of the
Admiralty and *Navy*) may enable them
to do right to the *Publick*, *Themfelves*,
and *Me*, by a timely rectifying of
any *Errors*, or Improvement of any
Truths, which *Time* may otherwife
render in themfelves lefs difcoverable,
or Us lefs folicitous in the looking
after them. In which confideration
I fhall (not gladly only, but) thank-
fully receive Intimations of any *Matters*
herein calling for *Amendment*; as well-
knowing how far from *infallible* his beft
endeavours muft be, that has to do with
a *Subject* so extenfive, various, and
complicate, as that of a *Navy*; and a
Navy circumftanc'd as this happens to
be within the limits of this *Chapter*.

But whatever (more or lefs) I may
meet with from better *Hands* towards
the improvement of this *Schitz*: Some-
what (I truft) of prefent utility may
(even as it is) be hoped for from it,

in the fo ample, freſh, and coſtly
Experiment (and to *England* moſt in-
ſtructive) which this *Paper* exhibits,
of the *Validity* of theſe three *Truths*
in its *Sea Oeconomy,* Viz.

Corol-   1.——**That** Integrity, *and general*
larys from (*but unpractic'd*) Knowledge, *are not alone*
the Pre- *ſufficient to conduct and ſupport a* Navy
miſes. *ſo, as to prevent its* Declenſion *into a*
State *little leſs unhappy, than the worſt*
that can befall it under the want *of* both.

2.——**That** *not much more* (*neither*)
is to be depended on, even from Experience *alone and* Integrity ; *unac-*
company'd with Vigour *of* Application,
Aſſiduity, Affection, Strictneſs *of* Diſcipline, *and* Method.

3.——**That** *it was a ſtrenuous* Conjunction *of all theſe* (*and that* Conjunction *only*) *that within half the* Time, *and*
leſs than half the Charge *it coſt the*
Crown *in the expoſing it,* had (*at the*
very inſtant of its unfortunate Lord's
Withdrawing from it) *rais'd the* Navy
                                   of

of England *from the loweſt ſtate of* Impotence, *to the moſt advanced ſtep towards a laſting and ſolid* Proſperity, *that* (all Circumſtances *conſider'd*) *this* Nation *had ever ſeen it at.*

And yet not ſuch; but that (even at this its *Zenith*) it both did and ſuffer'd ſufficient to *teach* us, that there is *Something* above both *That* and *Us*, that Governs the *World.*

To which (Incomprehen-
ſible) *alone be*
GLORY.

FINIS.

Index.

A

ACcount *of the* Monies *spent and* Services *perform'd upon the* Pro⟨po⟩sition, *Stated.*
Page 82
———*Its* Vouchers; *and* Observeables *there-from.* 83
Accounts *of the* Officers *of the* Navy, *their* Adjustment *provided for.* 24
———*Of the Charge of the* 30 New Ships *never made up.* 11, 70
———*Provision on that behalf by* Parliament *and otherwise yet ineffectual.* 12
———*Tho inculcated by the* King. 70
Admiralty-Management *alter'd by* K. Charles *April* 1679. 1

Vide-Commission.

B

Builders *and their* Assistants *in the Kings Yards,*—*Viz.*
———*Their present* List. 73
———*The* Surveyors *and* Estimators *of Works to be perform'd there.* 74
———*They*

Index.

C

Index.

Index.

D

Index.

P

Index.

Pro-

Index.

Index.

Index.

Index.

Index.

FINIS.